P9-CDW-582

GREAT THEMES IN SHORT FICTION

A Practical Teaching Guide

by
WILLIAM G. SWENSON

GREAT THEMES IN SHORT FICTION: A PRACTICAL TEACHING GUIDE
A Bantam Book / July 1975

All rights reserved.
Copyright © 1975 by Bantam Books, Inc.
This book may not be reproduced in whole or in part, by
mimeograph or any other means, without permission.
For information address: Bantam Books, Inc.

Published simultaneously in the United States and Canada

Bantam Books are published by Bantam Books, Inc. Its trade-
mark, consisting of the words "Bantam Books" and the por-
trayal of a bantam, is registered in the United States Patent
Office and in other countries. Marca Registrada. Bantam
Books, Inc., 666 Fifth Avenue, New York, New York 10019.

PRINTED IN THE UNITED STATES OF AMERICA

Table of Contents

List of Figures

GREAT THEMES IN SHORT FICTION

PREFACE

The minicourse/electives program is one that depends upon basic units of study easily adapted to short-term or semester course offerings. The program, built thematically upon important ideas found in literature, also allows the teacher to take advantage of the many diverse teaching aids currently available.

This Guide suggests to the teacher an English program that focuses on the reading of short stories containing themes of interest to the student today, along with an in-depth study of the art of the short story. Consequently, elements are brought together so that the course may center either on genre or on theme. Or, if the Guide is followed closely, the course may combine both approaches.

The short story offers a variety of appeals to both the teacher and the student. For students, these range from the joy of being able to finish a short evening assignment to the excitement of finding a theme and supporting it with elements discussed in class. Some students will react strongly to works of adventure and physical conflict; others will enjoy the more subtle interplay of theme and character development. To the teacher, the short story provides material for a wide-ranging study of both content and form. At all levels, and with students of varied learning abilities, the teacher can plan a meaningful program—from the simple study of basic purposes and themes found in the plot-centered story to the sophisticated structural analysis of character revelation. With some students outlining simple plots and others tracing the effective nuances of language in the building of character and tone, the teacher can plan an effective short story program that not only introduces the student to stimulating literature, but also shows the ingenious talent and discipline involved in the art of writing short fiction.

The adaptability of the minicourse/electives program allows the teacher to plan the course for 8, 10, 12, or 20 weeks. The careful, planned addition or reduction of suggested areas of study will maintain the effectiveness and the unity of the course.

Part I: SCOPE OF THE COURSE

One of today's most popular literary forms is the short story. From its beginnings the short story has been developed by master storytellers and literary artists. In their hands, the elements of plot, character, setting, diction, and theme have been blended to give us unforgettable short stories as well as a literary form that meets the varied needs of creative storytellers and students of human nature.

The course, "Great Themes in Short Fiction," will have two basic concerns—(1) to examine older and contemporary themes of universal interest to young people today, and (2) to deepen the students' appreciation of short story writing by gaining a knowledge of the basic elements of the short story and their handling by a wide range of authors.

A basic theme of interest to both junior and senior high school students is that of "coping with life." From the earliest short story writers to those practicing today, the characteristics and conflicts of individuals, both common and unique, have formed the basis for excellent short fiction. During the course three key strands that can be examined at both junior and senior high levels include:

Coping with one's problems
Coping with others
Coping with outside forces.

Each of these themes should suggest other strong thematic concerns of fiction today. For example, "coping with one's problems" can be stated as "the search for self-identity," "individuality and its consequences," or "growth to maturity." "Coping with others" brings to mind themes such as "revenge," "the individual vs. society," "games people play," and many others. "Coping with outside forces" can focus on works dealing with "man and technology," "man's struggle to

3

survive," and "romanticism and naturalism in short fiction." The instructor can use the three key themes presented in the Guide or arrange the study of short fiction around any number of ideas.

In order to have younger readers grasp the author's basic purpose and to have more mature readers state themes specifically and point out the many nuances in style, character development, and plot construction, the teacher must deal with the structural elements of the story. Basic and advanced ideas dealing with plot, character, setting, diction, and theme must be carefully presented to the students in the form of classroom and extracurricular activities. In this way the student will come to see that in short fiction form and content are brought together effectively by an author in complete control of his creative artistry.

Although basically a short story course, "Great Themes in Short Fiction" should not be solely a literature course. The teacher should continue to develop basic English skills related to the needs of each class. On the junior high level this might mean a continuing program of paragraph writing, sentence structure skills, and language skills. On the senior high level there might be a review of usage skills, a review of effective paragraph construction, and work on the literary composition.

Since the minicourse or electives program is limited both by length and scope, it is not possible to develop a complete skills mastery program usually associated with the year-long course. However, commitment to the minicourse program must include a departmental awareness of an ongoing skills program stressing levels of learning to be accomplished throughout the entire school experience.

Part II: SUGGESTED BASIC MATERIALS

Junior High School

Ten Modern American Short Stories. David A. Sohn, ed. New York: Bantam Books, Inc., 1965.

Ten Top Stories. David A. Sohn, ed. New York: Bantam Books, Inc., 1964.

Twenty Grand Short Stories. Ernestine Taggard, ed. New York: Bantam Books, Inc., 1963.

50 Great Short Stories. Milton Crane, ed. New York: Bantam Books, Inc., 1971.

Senior High School

50 Great American Short Stories. Milton Crane, ed. New York: Bantam Books, Inc., 1965.

50 Great Short Stories. Milton Crane, ed. New York: Bantam Books, Inc., 1971.

Additional Materials

To offer the student more supportive material, the following titles may be used to broaden and reinforce the unit "Great Themes in Short Fiction." These books provide stimulating, motivating reading that may be used in class to provide:

1. extra material for the teacher to meet the demands of differentiated learning abilities within the class
2. material for written work or extracurricular reading related to the unit
3. material for student-centered responses in the form of student-directed class forums, discussion panels, or oral reports

4. varied materials that form the basis for contract learning or learning-activity programs.

The Ballad of the Sad Cafe and Other Stories, C. McCullers
Big City Stories by Modern American Writers, T. and S. Cahill (eds.)
Collected Short Stories, A. Huxley
The Complete Short Stories of Mark Twain, C. Neider (ed.)
Devils and Demons, R. Serling (ed.)
Doctor Brodie's Report, J. Borges
50 Great Ghost Stories, J. Canning (ed.)
50 Great Horror Stories, J. Canning (ed.)
50 True Tales of Terror, J. Canning (ed.)
The Golden Apples of the Sun, R. Bradbury
Goodbye, Columbus, P. Roth
Great Tales of Horror, E. Poe
I Sing the Body Electric, R. Bradbury
The Long Valley, J. Steinbeck
Machineries of Joy, R. Bradbury
The Nick Adams Stories, E. Hemingway
Nine Stories, J. D. Salinger
Phineas, J. Knowles
Seven Masterpieces of Gothic Horror, R. Spector (ed.)
75 Short Masterpieces, R. Goodman (ed.)
Stories and Prose Poems, A. Solzhenitsyn
Stories of Five Decades, H. Hesse
Ten Times Black, J. Mayfield (ed.)
Timeless Stories for Today and Tomorrow, R. Bradbury (ed.)
We Be Word Sorcerers, S. Sanchez (ed.)
The World's Best Short Short Stories, R. Goodman (ed.)

*More difficult stories
Each of the above titles is available from Bantam Books, Inc.

Part III: PLANNING THE MINICOURSE/ ELECTIVES PROGRAM: BASIC CONSIDERATIONS

The successful course is almost always the result of meaningful learning experiences derived from careful, knowledgeable planning. The teacher can best plan for success by *maintaining sound, sensible goals and by being familiar with all materials to be taught.*

In the minicourse situation of 8, 10, 12, or 20 weeks the instructor must be sensitive to the time factor, particularly for those students who need aid in developing a sense of planning. While this is important on both junior and senior high school levels, it is seemingly more important to junior high planning, where more attention should be paid to the problems of *when* to do school work and *how* to accomplish it effectively. The shortened course of 8, 10, or 12 weeks does not mean that work must be covered faster, but rather that fewer works can be assigned for effective teaching and learning. The teacher must put himself in the role of the student when planning the course work. Therefore, even in a course dealing with short fiction, longer reports or term papers must be carefully devised and adequately presented with enough working time given to the student.

Careful, meaningful planning is the providing of works, grouped by similar or contrasting themes, in an order that allows the student time to carry out reading and writing assignments. In the shortened minicourse there is always the tendency to forge ahead with reading and cut time needed for written work and skills review. The instructor must experiment to discover which works should be discussed individually and which can be handled as a group. Also, there are works that can be assigned to individual students for in-class reporting while the entire class focuses on a total-group work. In the minicourse, especially where there is a wide range of reading abilities and interests, faster students should be encouraged to complete the work assigned and then carry out related assignments, ranging from the reading of other works by an author under discussion to exploring the library for critical evaluations.

The instructor should also plan for the orderly introduction, review, or continuation of English skills. In addition to the skills associated with reading and discussing literature, there are those that include writing, speaking, listening, and thinking. Here, a carefully developed departmental commitment to skills and their levels of accomplishment will aid the teacher in the planning of an integrated, ongoing program.

The instructor should carefully determine the nature of the course requirements if extracurricular writing assignments or related activities will be required. Then, reasonable course reading goals must be established, particularly in junior high school. The minicourse lends itself to the assignment of specific, short writings. These, in turn, provide opportunities for the review of sentence structure, paragraph development, research techniques, and library skills. The system of grading, for both classroom and extracurricular work, should be clear to the students at the beginning of the course.

In both the minicourse and the semester offering, the teacher should avoid the basic, often unwitting, weakness of the minicourse—the presentation of solely literary experiences. The effective English course must provide various experiential strands. By assessing students on the bases of past performance, diagnostic evaluations, and day-to-day classroom participation, the teacher can provide a variety of needed experiences.

To ensure that the minicourse and the semester elective relate to student interests and concerns, the teacher also should make use of supportive audio-visual materials—recordings, sound filmstrips, and motion pictures dealing with literature and short fiction. In many instances, there are students who possess the talent, interest, and means of making their own audio-visual materials for the course.

Part IV: GOALS/OBJECTIVES FOR THE COURSE

The minicourse/electives program built around a literary theme of importance to the young reader must offer the student a planned series of basic skills that will enable him to carry out written, oral, and reading activities. In addition, it must encourage him to face the important questions about his own existence that are posed by the works read and discussed in class.

To accomplish these goals, the following objectives are offered in both the cognitive (learning and skills) and affective (attitudes and feelings) domains. They may be expanded or reduced by the teacher to meet the needs of the specific class. To establish his own goals the teacher must ask, and answer, three basic questions:

1. What do I want to do?   (expectation)
2. How is this to be done most
   effectively?   (implementation)
3. When will I know it has been done?   (evaluation)

To improve the effectiveness of the learning experience, all goals should be stated in terms of *activities* wherein students respond to clearly defined, simply stated actions.

Course Objectives

I. Literature (Reading)

A. Basing his replies on past experiences, the student will list the types of conflict (physical, mental, spiritual) confronting people.
B. Using his experiences, the student will list the character traits that best lend themselves to literary treatment.

C. Using his experiences, the student will list the social situations that provide the best conflicts for literary treatment.

D. Using works read in class, the student will select a story using the following methods of character revelation and explain the author's use of this method to the class:

1. character revealed by author's description
2. character revealed by another character in the story
3. character revealed by his or her own words, actions, or thoughts
4. character revealed by the reactions of others.

E. After reading a work assigned in class, the student will select passages to be read and analyzed in which the author's use of words and sentence structure:

1. create a definite mood
2. reveal a character more effectively
3. increase or slow down the movement of the work
4. help build the overall tone of the work.

F. After reading a work *not* assigned previously, the student will develop his own theme statement and support it with textual references in a clear, well-organized paper.

G. During the reading of works in the course, the student will develop his own list of criteria for judging short fiction and then present it to the class for discussion.

H. Using the works read in class, the student will select a work that is built on the elements listed below and be prepared to show how the author uses each element successfully:

1. plot
2. setting
3. character
4. diction
5. theme.

I. Using a story selected for analysis by the teacher, the student will give examples of each of the following, where applicable:

1. protagonist
2. antagonist
3. foil

4. conflict
5. climax
6. foreshadowing
7. flashback
8. parallel scenes
9. symbolism or imagery.

J. Using a work assigned in class, the student will discuss the author's use of point of view and show how it affects the entire story.

K. Using works read in class, the student will select stories in which the setting is used to support each of the following and, in effective paragraphs, show how the setting is used to support:

1. theme
2. character revelation
3. plot.

L. Using the techniques for reading short fiction, the student will attempt to apply them to other genres and media for classroom discussion. These areas may include:

1. the novel
2. the drama
3. the television drama or television movie
4. the motion picture.

II. Writing

A. Using a theme topic given in class, the student will write at least one carefully organized paper of two or more paragraphs, identifying the following:

1. theme statement (controlling idea)
2. paragraph topic sentence
3. transitions
4. conclusion.

B. Using works read in class, the student will write a short literary theme using one or more of the following types of paragraphs:

1. illustration
2. definition

3. cause and effect
4. detail
5. comparison/contrast.

C. Using a work read in class, the student will select one element of the story and, using three critical works, will write a short, well-organized paper discussing professional opinions of the element. The student will use correct punctuation for quotations, proper footnote form, and proper bibliography form.

D. Selecting a person known to him or her, the student will write a short character sketch based on description, imagery, contrast, or incident. Then, after drawing up a theme, plot line, and character analysis based on the character sketch, the student will write a short fiction work built around the character.

E. Using the works read in class, the student will write a plot précis for each, citing the theme or purpose, and major elements used by the author.

III. Speaking

A. Using a short story not read in class, the student will prepare an oral analysis of the work to be given in class. Preparation for the talk will include:

1. a working outline
2. a detailed outline
3. note cards (if used during the talk).

Part V: TEACHING THE SHORT STORY

A course devoted to themes in short fiction on both the junior and senior high levels should attempt to (1) help students maturely discuss, both orally and in writing, the works they have read, (2) give the students the skills and awareness needed to read a story more effectively, and (3) show the relationship of the short story to other major literary types.

The short story course in junior high should not be the same course in the senior high. Too often the "teaching" of literature at every grade level, rather than the reading of literature, simply destroys the students' desire to go on with the unit. However, there are basic skills in handling plot, character, setting, diction, and theme that can help the younger reader understand a story better and discuss it more effectively. The more mature reader should be expected to "find" more in the short story. He should be aware of relationships between story elements, be more sensitive to the author's purpose and use of language, be more conscious of the development of style, and, possibly, be familiar with several literary philosophies of short story composition as well as different critical approaches. The teacher will be able to determine the necessity for, and depth of, skills teaching by the way the students handle the initial stories assigned for class reading.

One way of increasing a student's ability to handle short fiction is to look at each story in terms of both *content* and *form*. The importance of structural elements to the story itself can be seen in the following diagram:

(Fig. 1)

For instance, a comment on Poe's rationale for the short story's unity of purpose might help make clearer the importance of structure and form in the short story. By using a consistent approach to each story, the teacher can build within the student a method for careful reading. Of course, as students become more adept and skillful, more mature critical questions should be introduced to avoid a sterility that comes from being too methodical.

The statement of theme or purpose has created too many problems for the student. Too often he has come to look for "the moral" of the story. This ardent search often leads to a simplistic, moral statement that has very little to do with the work at hand. The younger reader should be able to state themes or purposes in clear terms based on his reading of the story. Often, the teacher can list with the class major themes and purposes, showing how many stories do not lend themselves to a clear thematic statement. For example, the class may discover something like the following:

Major Purpose	Possible Theme
1. To entertain (often non-thematic)	
a. the hero tale	man vs. nature
b. the humorous sketch	man vs. man
c. the mood or tone story	man vs. society
2. To reveal character	A weak man often seeks escape in dreams
3. To reveal basic human strengths or weaknesses	Without trust, man is doomed
4. To support, teach, or	Man is biologically unfit to

14

preach a specific philosophy, idea, or opinion	survive in the battle with nature
5. To make fun of some human characteristic, event, or institution	People are too unimaginative and gullible in their dealings with others
6. To reflect archetypal, mythic themes	The quest The king must die The search for the missing father

The teacher and the class may arrive at many other broad themes and purposes in a class discussion, and students should be encouraged to give examples of works read that support their findings. It should be noted that strong thematic statements simply cannot be made for many works, particularly those written for entertainment and amusement. For example, Connell's "The Most Dangerous Game" or Stephenson's "Leiningen Versus the Ants" are two wonderfully exciting, plot-centered action stories, the former using a "man vs. man" theme and the latter a "man vs. nature" idea. Students may pick up Leiningen's motto that the human mind can outwit any force of nature for a specific theme statement, but to go further will destroy the work and force the student to come up with a silly statement. However, the more mature student should be prodded to look more deeply into some works, deceptively simple and straightforward, to find more meaningful statements about life. For example, James Thurber's "The Secret Life of Walter Mitty" cannot be explained simply by saying it is a work dealing with "man vs. woman" or that the theme concerns one man's escape from reality into a world of dreams. Careful reading of Thurber's choice of scenes, words, and names will reveal the pathetic situation of a weak man at the mercy of not only a demanding, powerful woman, but also an awesome, complex, modern, technological world. This poor soul, who bungles his way quietly through life, continues to reveal his inadequacies in the heroic escapes of his dreams. In Mitty we see Thurber's comic-pathetic answer to the nineteenth century hero.

One way of getting students to respond to the sometimes difficult task of stating themes clearly is to use the "funnel approach," whereby themes may be stated in degrees of sophistication dependent on student experience, insight, and investigation. Pictorially, the approach may be diagrammed:

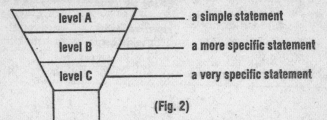

(Fig. 2)

Using this approach a short story such as Jack London's "To Build a Fire" would elicit a variety of responses. These might include the following:

Level A—Man vs. nature. (a simple statement calling for basic plot reading)

Level B—Man, unable to cope with the unseen forces of nature, will be destroyed. (a closer reading of the story in which the reader sees the contrast between the man and the dog and is aware of the underlying power of nature as seen in the immediate effects upon the man)

Level C—London, supporting the biological determinism found in the philosophy of the naturalistic writer, shows how man is unfit to survive the irrational, instinctive forces of a hostile environment. [a careful reading of the story and an analysis of the unnamed man (reason), the dog (instinct), and the relentless background, coupled with insights gained by reading about the author and the views of the naturalists in the early decades of the twentieth century]

These sample responses call for increasingly sophisticated insights into a work and scrutiny of the author's use of theme, character, plot, setting, and tone. Such a growth in mature reading might be a goal started in the junior high school course (based on readings suitable for the younger reader) and carried to fruition in the senior high school.

Characters, and the ways in which they are revealed,

should be studied very carefully at the junior high level. Attention must be paid to the more subtle methods of characterization, as more sophisticated stories are read. These methods include:

1. Symbols and images
   a. names, or lack of names
   b. clothing
   c. physical attributes (glasses, weak eyes, eagle nose, etc.)
   d. colors

2. Character types
   a. protagonist
   b. antagonist
   c. foils or contrasting characters
   d. stereotypes
   e. archetypal-mythological types (i.e. the hero, the trickster, the wanderer)

The students, in their growing awareness of character development and change, will see the relationship that exists between character and theme in the more sophisticated stories.

At first, most students will be attracted to the plot-centered story that makes few demands on the reader. Unfortunately, influenced by the idea-less, action-filled plots of the average television show, the students will too often be satisfied with getting a shallow idea of what happened. The teacher should work to have the students identify the overall plot movement (noting the time involved, the changes of setting, the repeated incidents, and the conclusion) and indicate its relationship to the other basic elements of the story—setting, character, tone, and theme. There should be an understanding of the basic movement of the short story (Fig. 3).

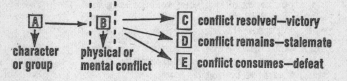

(Fig. 3)

Quite often, the plot movement can be seen as following the familiar dramatic plot line (Fig. 4). Arthur Conan Doyle's Sherlock Holmes stories are good examples of this.

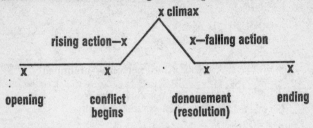

(Fig. 4)

According to this, Arthur Conan Doyle's "The Adventure of the Speckled Band" would be plotted as follows:

1. Opening—young lady in distress comes to Holmes.
2. Conflict begins—Helen Stoner's story and the visit from Dr. Roylott.
3. Rising action—Holmes' inspection of the death room and the surrounding land.
4. Climax—Holmes, through the powers of deduction, solves the crime and plans to trap the guilty.
5. Falling action—Holmes and Watson wait in the death room to catch the murderer.
6. Denouement—Holmes reveals to Watson the clues that gave him the solution to the mystery.
7. Ending—disposition of the murderer.

The students, in their growing awareness of character development and plot incidents, will see that important events happen quickly in the short story as opposed to the novel and play; the change of character may be seen in a few words or a hinted action. As plot is studied more closely, the student will come across the following aspects of development:

1. Variations
   a. "non-plotted" character sketch
   b. surprise ending
   c. cyclical plot
   d. stream-of-consciousness movement (see Hemingway's "A Way You'll Never Be")

2. Expository techniques
   a. *In medias res* (in the middle)
   b. frame story
   c. flashback
   d. foreshadowing
   e. contrast
   f. parallel scenes

3. Point of View
   a. omniscient author (third person)—unlimited
   b. third person—limited
   c. main character (first person)—limited
   d. minor character (first person)—limited

Many students pay little attention to the author's use of setting, simply stating that the story "could have taken place anywhere." While there are stories that make little use of setting, often students miss the influence of setting on character ("To Build a Fire") or on theme (most of Poe's works). Constant practice in examining setting will help the student keep track of place names, repeated scenes, symbols (e.g. Poe's vacant, eye-like windows in the cracked, skull-like mansion in "The Fall of the House of Usher"), time sequences (particularly the use of dawn and late night), and the seasons (e.g. the symbolic use of summer and winter in Knowles' "A Turn with the Sun"). A careful, ongoing study of these elements—character, plot, and setting—should not only increase the students' appreciation of short fiction, but also arm them with advanced skills to use with all types of fiction.

Finally, the student should become more aware of an author's use of story elements to create a specific tone or mood. Obvious examples of a definite tone can be found in the works of Poe and Ambrose Bierce. However, there is a subtle development of tone that increases our awareness in stories like Walter Van Tilburg Clark's "The Portable Phonograph" (the moral tone accompanying man's final days is strengthened by the numerous religious symbols) and Benet's "By the Waters of Babylon" (mythical and spiritual tones that accompany the ritual are captured by the use of archetypal themes and characters as well as mythological symbols and allusions). Using appropriate stories, the teacher, aided by meaningful, provocative questions, can lead students to a discovery of tone in the following:

1. The author's use of language
   a. specific words that affect the emotions
   b. sentence style (grammatical elements)
   c. repetition
   d. contrast
   e. symbols

2. The author's use of story elements
   a. setting descriptions
   b. portrayal of characters
   c. arrangement of plot incidents

Exactly where "teaching" the short story begins and ends at the junior and senior high level cannot be dogmatically set down. The teacher should discover as soon as possible, through a diagnostic story or two, exactly what the students know and don't know about reading the short story. The teacher should then plan units around the learning he/she feels is necessary, meaningful, and possible for his/her own classes. Once this is set up both teacher and student can begin to enjoy the wonderful world of short fiction.

The teacher might consider the use of a "Checklist for Short Stories" (Fig. 5) and the "Super (fill in your own name) Short Story Chart for Beginners and Pros" (Fig. 6) to help the students track, rate, and summarize the works read in class. Kept up faithfully by the student, each device will enable students to recall works read throughout the unit.

Checklist for Short Stories

Title:

Author:

1. The PLOT (check where applicable)

- [ ] clear
- [ ] believable
- [ ] true-to-life
- [ ] logical
- [ ] good ending

- [ ] confusing
- [ ] contrived
- [ ] unreal
- [ ] too manipulated
- [ ] poor ending

2. The CHARACTERS

- [ ] true-to-life
- [ ] individuals
- [ ] complex
- [ ] related to other elements

- [ ] unreal
- [ ] stereotypes
- [ ] too simple
- [ ] not essential to the story

3. The SETTING (check, if appropriate to the story)

- [ ] authentic
- [ ] true to the period
- [ ] necessary

- [ ] not believable
- [ ] distorted
- [ ] unnecessary

4. The THEME or PURPOSE (check where appropriate)

- [ ] To entertain
- [ ] To depict man's struggles (explain briefly)
- [ ] To depict man's basic characteristics (explain briefly)
- [ ] To teach, instruct, or point out (explain briefly)
- [ ] To reveal a specific feeling or mood (explain briefly)

(Fig. 5)

Super ___ Short Story Chart for Beginners and Pros						
Title	Author	Character(s)	Setting	Basic Plot	Purpose	Key Features

(Fig. 6)

Part VI: USING THE MATERIALS

Many of the short stories suggested for this course will be discussed here in terms of the course goals and specific themes. The teacher and the student have available to them a great deal of critical material on many of these stories, and such material can be worked into class discussions and class writings.

The analysis of the following works seeks to (1) place the individual work within a theme of the course (content), and (2) suggest elements of the story that should be discussed in terms of understanding the craft of the short story writer (form). These stories may serve as examples for the many others available in the anthologies. The questions presented with each analysis are included as discussion starters. After a few stories have been read and discussed in class, the students should be encouraged to provide the questions.

The specific placement of works within the unit is only one possibility for the course. The teacher is encouraged to work with more stories, develop his own analyses, and present them to the class in a way that promotes meaningful, effective learning.

The Short Story in the Senior High School

"The Tale" by Joseph Conrad

Source: *50 Great Short Stories* edited by David A. Sohn
Recommended level: senior high school

Content—Discussing Theme

As an introduction to the unit, and a re-introduction to the short tale as the well-told story, "The Tale" should provide the teacher with material to begin discussion of the short story. Students should be encouraged to attack each story with a definite plan, which includes the following:

1. Read the story *twice*, first to get an idea of the situation, and second, to focus on the elements of the story.
2. Look up words you do not know and cannot figure out in context.
3. What is the main situation? (plot)
4. What are the characters like? What are noticeable conflicts, contrasts?
5. What is the major conflict in the story?
6. Does the main character change during the story? How?
7. Is the setting important to the action, the description of characters, or the overall mood?
8. Is there special emphasis placed on the following:
   a. names, colors, places
   b. times of the year
   c. poems, titles, or quotes used in the story
   d. distinctive physical assets or liabilities?
9. What does the story reveal about life that involves more than just the characters?

Because of the style and vocabulary, a Joseph Conrad story is a difficult one to begin with, even in high school. However, the student should be introduced to the more difficult story and be expected to analyze the work with some insight. "The Tale" is a typical Conrad work dealing with a man's discovery of his true self. The story, like others, hinges on making a decision which involves the individual's outward sense of duty and his inner fears. The Commander in "The Tale" must decide to either accept or reject the Northman's story. However, caught up in an environment that heightens one's senses (where the familiar becomes unfriendly, and the innocent can be deadly) the Commander makes a grave error in the struggle between duty and reason, between inner fears and the observable truth. This moral error destroys the Commander's inner peace and contentment and his self-doubts affect all areas of his life. He has gained a terrible knowledge of himself. He speaks with a "dead, equable tone" and sees that " ... duty demands more from a person and that it contains. ... An infinity of absolution ..." but he cannot be absolved. (p. 372)

Form—Elements of the Story

Plot

In the plot-centered tale (the more traditional type of short story) the reader can find a clear situation—a character encounters a problem (the conflict), attacks the problem, and then either succeeds, fails, or emerges untouched by the problem. Conrad, a complex storyteller, involves the Commander in several conflicts and reveals them to the reader by using the "frame story" (i.e. a story-within-a-story). The Commander, engaged in a conflict with a woman who seems to be rejecting his protestations of love "while her being vibrated yet with conflicting emotions," (p. 371), tells the inner story about the costly incident at sea during the war. Both the inner story and the thinly suggested outer story reveal the consequences of the conflicts that have engulfed the hapless Commander.

Characters

Although the plot is important, it is a vehicle for the depiction of the Commander and his discovery. The reader should see him as a person who is quiet by nature, unbending, imperious, and as a man who has built up an image of himself as a man of honor dedicated to sincerity, frankness, and passion. During his war service he comes to see himself as the defender of "... simple right, common decency, all humanity of feeling, every scruple of conduct." (p. 383)

Nevertheless, darker forces are at work and he is attacked from within. Although he feels that "Everything should be open in love and war," (p. 376) life will not have it so. The Commander's fear of suddenly dying at the hands of an unseen force mounts, and this dread turns into hatred for the neutrals. His world is turned around, and fear changes the truth into a lie; the simplicity of life becomes distressingly complex. As Conrad says, "But his commanding officer was in revolt against the murderous stealthiness of methods and the atrocious callousness of complicities that seemed to taint the very source of men's deep emotions and noblest activities; to corrupt their imagination which builds up the final conceptions of life and death. He suffered——" (p. 376) The agony and suffering brought about by his fears and doubts blind the Commander to the Northman. He yields to his worst fears and finds his reason distorted by them as he:

1. accepts the circumstantial evidence of the wreckage and the bells not sounding
2. is blinded by his growing hatred of neutrals
3. is disgusted by the surface innocence of the Northman's story
4. is unduly influenced by the Northman's drinking
5. is blinded by the Northman's attempt to make money while he is fighting a war.

The self-doubt and torture that become the Commander's inheritance are heightened by the woman's reaction and her "Oh, my poor, poor——" (p. 385), and he can do no more than quietly leave her.

Setting

The wartime background provides the battleground for the forces at work within the Commander. His taut feelings, overt fears, and uncertainties work to strengthen his prejudices against the Northman. At the same time the thick fog enveloping the men, the ship, and the world around them creates disorder in the moral world of the Commander as: "Mist is deceitful, the dead luminosity of the fog is irritating." (p. 375)

Tone

The moral darkness experienced by the Commander is reinforced by the somber quality of the frame story. In the opening paragraphs heaviness and darkness flow through Conrad's phrases ("without colour," "dying out," "framed rigidly," "gathering shades" p. 371). The woman on the couch is no more than a dark, shadowy figure, a "suggestion;" the darkness covers the unpleasantness that exists between them. The return to the frame at the end picks up the mood as "Her eyes put two gleams in the deep shadow of the room." (p. 385) Conrad builds his mood by appealing to the senses of the reader.

In a preface to the *Nigger of the Narcissus* (1897), Conrad made the following statements about the art of the short story writer:

> And Art itself may be defined as a single-minded attempt to render the highest kind of justice to the visible universe, by bringing to light the truth, manifold and one, underlying its every aspect.

> . . . My task which I am trying to achieve is, by the power of the written word to make you hear, to make you feel—it is, before all, to make you see.

Questions

1. What do we learn about the character of the Commander?
2. How does his character affect his action?
3. Why does Conrad use this title?
4. Why is the woman in the story? In what ways is she necessary?
5. What is the mood of the Commander? How is this reinforced by the elements of the story?

"Theft" by Katherine Anne Porter

Source: *50 Great Short Stories* edited by Milton Crane
Recommended level: senior high school

Content—Discussing Theme

Unlike the plot-centered, traditional short story, the character sketch or revelation provides different problems for the reader. The author who chooses to reveal a character will focus on specific aspects of character—dialogue, appearance, thoughts, and reactions. The reader accustomed to strong plot lines will often miss the subtleties and implied meanings that bring out a character fully. Often the character will be revealed as he reacts, or fails to react, to a relatively insignificant incident.

The important point to get across to the student is that in the hands of a skillful writer the character revelation short story is not simply a "My Favorite Uncle" thematic essay. Katherine Anne Porter, as well as the other writers studied in this course, uses her consummate skill to deal with a universal aspect of life. The well-written character sketch involves the reader in an important discovery about life and living. To do this, the author often resorts to more subtle uses of language. Images and symbols present ideas. A gesture or word is used instead of a more obvious physical action. The "meaning" of the work is caught not so much in what the character *does*, but rather what the character *is*.

These points come out clearly in the very subtle "Theft." A nameless character finds herself forced to look at her own existence and her failures in life and love. We know little about her and we must guess about what has happened to her and where she lives. The intimate knowledge of her that we gain comes from a variety of sources: the three men she talks with, the youths she overhears while riding in a taxi, the confrontation with the janitress, and, finally, the implied meaning of the purse itself. A sad, dismal background adds to the picture. We see a woman, proud that nothing has been stolen from her (although she has never locked a door), discover through the theft of her purse that she herself has stolen all of her chances for future happiness and love. The purse, a symbol of her very life, drying out as she is drying out, forces her to think to herself, "I was right not to be afraid of any thief but myself, who will end up by leaving me nothing." (p. 188) The theft, the letters received by Roger and herself, and the evening in the rain provoke within her an almost transcendental insight that brings to her and the reader a pathos and a new awareness of the ironies of life.

Form—Elements of the Story

Plot

While essentially plotless, there are several ways in which Porter unifies her story and forces the reader to put together what has been only suggested. The complete story, spanning one night and the following morning, is told in the third person by the main character who reflects on the previous evening (flashback) to re-trace the steps that lead up to the theft of her purse. The story is plotted as follows:

1. The discovery of the theft and the recollection of putting the purse down.
2. The recollection of (a) the previous evening with Camilo, Roger, and Bill, which leads to the reading of her letter, (b) the actual theft by the janitress, and (c) the initial confrontation with the janitress moments before.
3. Back to the cold coffee at the table, the woman reflects upon the return of the purse and the meaning of her life.

In addition to this cyclic action, the story is unified by the omnipresent number three. During the course of the remembered evening and the traumatic morning the woman:

1. meets with three men
2. hears three boys discussing their feeling about marriage
3. thinks about three hats (Camilo's flashy but ruined hat, Roger's protected hat, and Eddie's misshapen but comfortable hat)
4. hears about Bill's three rehearsals
5. remembers she won't get a check for three days
6. walks down three flights of stairs to the basement.

This haunting refrain and the use of the word "purse" throughout the story tighten a work that cannot be unified by action.

Character

The unnamed woman is revealed clearly through the story in several ways:

1. She reviews plays for a living and has written an unsuccessful act for Bill's play.
2. She knew an Eddie, who might have written her the letter.
3. She was friendly with Roger in the past, but now he has chosen a girl named Stella.
4. Camilo is a passing fancy who has no interest in her, but likes to show her off.

29

5. She has the unfortunate knack of turning away from people, places, and plans ("In this moment she felt that she had been robbed of an enormous number of valuable things, whether material or intangible ... the long patient suffering of dying friendships and the dark inexplicable death of love ..." (p. 187)

The three men she meets in the story provide contrasts with the woman and run the gamut from the flashy gigolo (Camilo), to the protective, independent, amiable friend (Roger), to the incapable, self-pitying weakling (Bill). The first cannot love and return to her; the second cannot wait for her love any longer; the third could never offer her love.

She hears a young boy saying that "When I get married, it won't be jus' for getting married, I'm gonna marry for *love*, see?" (p. 184) Moments later, a young girl passes by discussing her recent breakup with a friend. The woman cannot escape thinking about love, lost love, and love never to be claimed. She has, through her ways and actions, stolen her chances for happiness.

Setting

The woman's unsettling discovery is made amidst surroundings that are equally dismal. Everyone in the story is poor, and the rain pours down incessantly ". . . changing the shapes of everything, and the colors." (p. 184) The loss of her purse provokes startling insights into her wasted life, and pushes her into the dreadful confrontation with the janitress, a hellish-looking person with a face "streaked with coal dust" and "hot flicking eyes." (pp. 185 & 186)

Tone

The somber mood of the story is the product of the setting, the essential loneliness of the person, and the pathetic truth that is revealed through the deeper meaning of the lost purse.

Questions
1. In what ways does Porter make use of the title?
2. What do we know, and not know, about the woman?
3. What purpose do the other characters serve?
4. How do we learn more by what has been omitted from the story?

5. Why is the purse so important?
6. How does the setting add to the story?

"By the Waters of Babylon"
by Stephen Vincent Benet

Source: *50 Great American Short Stories* edited by Milton Crane
Recommended level: senior high school

Content—Discussing Theme

"By the Waters of Babylon" can be discussed on several levels. John, the priest's son, copes with his own problem (the need to know the truth) and the problems of his society (learning about the past in order to grow into the future). The various themes of the work may be stated as follows:

1. The search for the truth (knowledge).
2. The initiation into manhood.
3. The struggle between knowledge and morality.
4. The need to control progress ("Perhaps, in the old days, they ate knowledge too fast." p. 260)

As the class follows the adventures of John, who solves problems for his people as he satisfies his own needs, they should see that a closer reading of a story turns a seemingly simple, plot-centered adventure tale into a deeper story containing strong universal themes dealing with man and his destiny.

Form—Elements of the Story

Plot

Benet has cloaked his meaningful story in the excitement of an adventure. Here we find an indomitable protagonist (the hero) who overcomes early obstacles, goes on a perilous journey, finds the secret treasure (here, it takes the form of knowledge), and returns in glory to claim his reward (here, he takes not a kingdom, but his father's role in guiding his people).

The first person, limited point of view helps the straightforward story by placing the reader within the main character. By adding the clues, as John sees them, the author lets the reader guess, and finally discover the truth when John does.

Character

John, whose very name means "God's gracious gift," plays a role found in literature dealing with the themes of man's existence and growth. He is the new leader of his people, the one who brings discovered knowledge and renewed life to his followers. He will supplant his father and bring insights gained through a perilous journey. In this light, and fitting the mytho-poetic nature of the story, John resembles the classic Greek hero (see Bantam's teaching guide, *The Mythmakers*) in the following ways:

1. He is not a common man (the son of the priest).
2. He passes an early test of courage by fearlessly touching the metal his father gives him.
3. He undergoes a long, perilous journey.
4. He is guided by the gods (note the eagle omen).
5. He returns to glory.
6. He has a magic weapon (not a material aid, but the "fire" in his mind that seeks the truth).

Also, John is at times part Indian; his journey resembles the puberty rites of certain American Indian tribes. During these rites a young initiate fasted, went to the wilderness alone, waited for the mystic vision of the Great Spirit to speak to him, and then reported back to the tribe's elders for acceptance into the tribe as a man.

Setting

The setting is vital to the story in several ways. The rise and fall of great civilizations is seen in three instances in the story. New York, the center of modern technology and culture, reduced to ruins because man's knowledge outstripped his morality, supports a basic theme of the work. Great cultures of the past are alluded to in the statue of the bird (Egypt) and the vivid painting of the yellow flowers (Van Gogh's "Sunflowers").

To add suspense to the story and involve the reader in the

main character's quest, Benet gives clues to the setting which can either be clear or obscure, depending on one's knowledge of New York City. For example, we find the following:

1. Magic numbers and names—the building numbers and street names.
2. UBTREAS and ASHING—the *Subtreas*ury Building in the financial district (Wall Street), and downtown New York (with a statue of George *Washing*ton on the steps).
3. The cavernous building with tunnels and the sky painted on the ceiling—Grand Central Station in midtown New York.
4. Lincoln, Biltmore, Moses—probably signs denoting the old Lincoln Hotel, the Biltmore Hotel, and Robert Moses, the building planner whose name adds to the overall tone.

Tone

Benet's tale of adventure and his themes dealing with mankind's rise and fall are given a sense of the mysterious past by his use of archetypal-mythological themes and motifs. These motifs include the association of the boy with three arrows and his protection of the deer (the allusion is to Apollo, the hunter and god of truth), the eagle omen (from Zeus), and the quest. In addition, the attempt to relate John and his father to the mystical American Indian rites of puberty, gives the story a spiritual essence and captures the sense of the past.

The feeling of the primitive, which is built up to surprise the reader who has not deciphered the clues by the end, is carried to the reader by Benet's style. The repetition of the short declarative sentence with a predominant subject-verb-object pattern captures the rhythm of the chant and builds a "You Tarzan-Me Jane" style associated with primitive, uneducated man. The careful placement of these elements creates a contrast at the end when the reader discovers that the story takes place in the near future, not the distant past (note the similar ending, and locale, in Bouille's *Planet of the Apes*).

Questions

1. What is the significance of the title?

2. What is the nature of John's society? How is this revealed?
3. What are John's basic character traits? How do they influence him?
4. What social figures do John and his father represent?
5. What knowledge did John gain from his journey and from his father?
6. How does Benet attract the reader's attention and hold it in the story?
7. Who are other writers concerned with these or similar themes, and what have they written?

"Soldiers of the Republic" by Dorothy Parker

Source: *50 Great American Short Stories* edited by Milton Crane
Recommended level: senior high school

Content—Discussing Theme

Dorothy Parker's vivid portrait of men, little men, at war presents us with a familiar theme of men-at-war and the terrible effects of war upon the innocent. Reminiscent of Hemingway's "Old Man at the Bridge," this work is a plotless character sketch of poor farmers and peasants snatching a few hours of rest and companionship in a Spanish cafe during the bloody civil war of the 1930's.

Caught up in a ruthless war they know little about (note the early Sunday morning bombing of Valencia and the reported bombing of men, women, and children in the crowded bullring), the people display a nobility and "humanness" to the emotionally moved first-person narrator of the story. Filled with Hemingway's "grace under pressure," the patrons of the cafe reveal:

1. courage, and the refusal to crack under the threat of enemy bombs (pp. 261-2),
2. pride in their appearance, despite the difficulty of the times (note the patches in the baby's dress and the wife's lamenting the loss of mending thread),
3. a deep love of family (note the parents' joy in their baby and the six soldiers' concern for their loved ones),

34

4. dignity (the soldiers, lacking all social amenities and facing death in battle, pay for the women's drinks).

Form—Elements of the Story

Setting

Valencia, Spain during the Spanish Civil War is like most settings in wartime. Times are hard; the comforts of life are missing, or difficult to obtain (note how the waiter covets the ice); people live under the constant threat of death; and the future has to be lived in the present. Even the evening can be menacing as Parker describes the night as "... the quick, new dark that leaps down without dusk on the day." (p. 261)

Characters

Amidst the uncertainties and the dreariness of wartime life, it is the nameless people who teach the narrator a new meaning of courage. The narrator, and her silent companion, can only observe the "little" people caught up in the cataclysm with nothing left but their love of life and each other. After the morning attack, they crowd the cafe to find companionship, "... chatting of small, gay matters, all talking at once, all hearing and answering." (p. 262)

The small man and his wife take joy in their infant son, for whom the mother has sacrificed. Surrounded by death, she is again filled with life. The six farmers who sit with the women need to talk in order to relieve their tension and anxieties. They live each day close to death (they light grenades and cigarettes with the same yellow rope), but their concerns are for their families and their friends who have been swept into the frenzied attacks. And, in the midst of their pain and suffering, they do not forget to pay for the ladies' drinks.

Contrasting the silent, seemingly shocked narrator is the Swedish girl who "... has seen and heard too much to be knocked into silence." (p. 265) Dignity, courage, love, fear, and anxiety are not strangers to her. She has had the experiences; she has been initiated. Her only reply to the narrator's embarrassed comments on fashions in the cafe is, "Please?" which forces the uninitiated narrator into silence.

Tone

This subtle story with its keen observations and understatement forces the reader to examine the narrator, who seeks anonymity in the repeated use of "we," and to compare her to the others in the cafe. In this way the quiet strength and endurance of the people surge through the story up to the important last line.

Questions
1. What is the value of the title, if any?
2. What do we learn about the narrator?
3. What is the purpose behind the many comments made about dress in the cafe?
4. What kind of people are observed in the cafe?
5. What role does the setting play?
6. What is the importance of the last sentence?

"The Masque of the Red Death"
by Edgar Allan Poe

Source: *50 Great Short Stories* edited by Milton Crane
Recommended level: senior/junior high school

Content—Discussing Theme

Most students in senior high will have experienced a Poe story before and will be familiar with Poe's themes and motifs. They should recall that Poe's tales of ratiocination (his detective stories) and his gothic stories were written to fill the reader with terror, fright, and awe. To do this, Poe repeatedly uses several motifs that include the following:

1. the death of a beautiful woman,
2. burial alive,
3. madness,
4. the return from the dead,
5. isolation.

Students familiar with Poe's purpose and use of these motifs should then become familiar with Poe's philosophy of composition as well as the genre of the gothic romance. In his review of Hawthorne's *Twice-Told Tales*, which appeared in *Graham's Magazine* in May 1842, Poe wrote, "The tale proper, in my opinion, affords unquestionably the fairest field for the exercise of the loftiest talent, which can be afforded by the wide domains of mere prose." He goes on to say, "I need only here say, upon this topic, that in almost all classes of composition, the unity of effect or an impression is a point of the greatest importance."[1] The following are essential elements of the short story based on one effect:

1. It should be able to be read in one sitting.
2. It must be a totality.
3. The first sentence should aim at the purpose.
4. All words in the story should be aimed at the preconceived effect.
5. Terror, passion, or horror are effective themes to use in the tale of effect.

Poe carried out his ideas in the gothic short story. Students should be encouraged to investigate Romanticism and the gothic romance. They might also become interested in the early writers of this offshoot of the Romantic Movement. These would include Horace Walpole (*Castle of Otranto*, 1764), William Beckford (*Vathek*, 1786), Ann Radcliffe (*The Mysteries of Udolpho*, 1794), Mary Shelley (*Frankenstein*, 1817), and Charles Brockden Brown.

Form—Elements of the Story

Plot

The plot supports Poe's attempt to fill the reader with terror by moving along quickly. A plague develops and Prince Prospero takes to his castle with one thousand revelers. There they pass the time at elaborate parties, attempting to defy the marauding red death. However, during a lavish masquerade party, death enters as a reveler and soon takes over the Prince's little kingdom.

Characters

Along with setting, character is most important in "The Masque of the Red Death." Prince Prospero changes as he

---

[1] Perry Miller, ed., *Major Writers of America* (New York: Harcourt Brace & World, 1966), p. 234.

becomes the victim of the red death he has tried so hard to defeat. In the beginning, described as a happy, wise, fearless, and eccentric ruler, the Prince is tied to the dominant image of redness in the story as Poe says, "His plans were bold and fiery . . ." and later ". . . his brow reddened with rage." (p. 142) From the very beginning Prospero is touched with a redness that he seeks to escape. Like many of Poe's characters, Prospero is considered mad by some of his followers ("There were some who would have thought him mad." p. 140).

The partygoers complete the picture of madness within the enclosed castle ("Be sure they were grotesque." p. 140) as they passed their time in revelry, attempting to fight off the inevitable. Dressed in their "madman fashions" and referred to as "dreams" by Poe, they add to the fantasy and the surreal picture within the castle.

The end comes to the Prince and his followers as the masked figure (the masque of the red death) reveals himself just before the pealing of the twelfth chime at midnight. By this time the fear of the revelers has even affected the proud, defiant Prince, and the black-garbed, blood-covered figure with a mask like a "stiffened corpse" (p. 142) brings the inevitable plague to the palace of safety.

Setting

It is the setting that Poe uses most effectively in many of his stories. As Prince Prospero seals up the castle ("All these and security were within. Without was the 'Red Death.' " p. 139), the students should see Poe's motif of burial alive. Within the castle, they should also note how each of the seven rooms is a unique cell, set off from the others by a twisting hallway. These rooms become the dominant architectural image of the story. Perhaps Poe used seven to remind us of the seven ages of man or maybe he is paying homage to the archetypal-mythological seventh cycle of the moon during which the fertility king was sacrificed. All seven are oddly colored from a blue to a black. Of the seven rooms, three are connected to the color red. Also, the blue room is referred to as the easternmost (the beginning—life) and the black is the westernmost (the end—death). This last room is the most carefully described, and it is the one that spreads fear among the revelers. This room, resembling a coffin and being the abode of death itself, adds to Poe's purpose as he paints the following picture:

> ... the effect of the fire-light that streamed upon the dark hangings through the blood-tinted panes, was ghastly in the extreme, and produced so wild a look upon the countenances of those who entered, that there were few of the company bold enough to set foot within its precincts at all. (p. 140)

The black clock in the deathroom ticks off the time left to the Prince and his company. The masked figure draws Prince Prospero from the blue room through each of the others to his death in the velvet-lined black chamber.

Tone

Poe's selective use of words, his saturation technique of keeping the same images before the reader's eye, and his use of contrast create the desired effects. In the opening paragraph, with its short, story-controlling first sentence, Poe uses the following sets of tone words:

> Red Death-pestilence
> devastated-fatal-hideous
> blood-redness-blood-bleeding-scarlet

The final sentence, emphasizing the Red Death, simply expands on the opening, and the cycle has been completed.

Irony through contrast is an often repeated ingredient in the Poe story. The Prince's name recalls prosperity and good fortune in a tale of horrible death. The situation—a land devastated by the plague, and a lonely castle where revelry and wild abandon reign—adds to the macabre feeling, and the use of the word "Masque" reminds us immediately of masquerade parties, the dark figure of death, and Prince Prospero's futile attempt to hide from the inevitable touch of death.

Questions

1. Why does Poe use the word "Masque" in the title?
2. How does Poe observe a unified effect in the story?
3. How does Poe involve the reader's senses? Why?
4. Why, in a short work, does Poe spend so much time describing the inside of the castle?

5. What specific Poe situations are used in this story to create a particular feeling? In what other Poe stories have you found similar situations?

6. Using this story as a typical one, what would you say about Poe's ideas for writing a short story?

"To Build a Fire" by Jack London

Source: *50 Great American Short Stories* edited by Milton Crane

Recommended level: senior high school

Content—Discussing Theme

Jack London's "To Build a Fire" is a work that can be read on several levels. Basically a vivid re-creation of a man freezing to death, the story is seen by the less mature student as merely the familiar "man vs. nature" story without much of the action usually found in the conflict story. To the careful reader the story depicts a more meaningful conflict between a relentless, unfeeling, hostile environment and Man. The wider view will come to mind when the student notices (1) that the man in the story is not given a name, and therefore has no specific identity, (2) that the omnipresent dog, described always in terms of its instincts, experiences the same hardships as the man, and (3) that London emphasizes the man as a creature of reason who lacks imagination and therefore cannot truly cope with his world. Finally, a discussion of naturalism, either inspired by the teacher or discussed by a student in a report, will reveal the source of London's theme statement and treatment of character. A knowledge of naturalism—biological, social, and economic determinism—along with the historical-literary backgrounds of the movement will give the student another critical dimension for the study of succeeding works.

Form—Elements of the Story

Plot

The relatively simple plot—a man travels from point A to point B, meets obstacles along the way, makes a mistake, and succumbs to the excessive cold—exists basically as a structural necessity for the more important battle between reason and instinct. The threat posed by hidden water springs and the quick freezing of hands when the man eats his lunch give clues to the movement of the story and the eventual outcome. The use of parallel scenes adds unity to the story structure and contrast to the action. The dog falls through the ice and survives because it is conditioned by instinct and natural selection. The man later falls through the ice and is doomed when he panics and unwittingly builds his fire beneath a snow-laden tree. There are two fires built in the story. In the first scene, the fire is built, the man eats, and his confidence grows. In the second, he is unable to keep the fire alive, and his confidence is destroyed.

The third person (omniscient viewpoint) is used effectively by London. The view we get is gradually telescoped as the forces of nature become invincible. For example, the opening paragraphs present a panoramic view of the limitless white expanse of the Yukon, the undulating, hairline trail that stretches endlessly, and the speck that is man. As the story progresses, the view narrows to the man and finally to his frozen hands vainly clutching burning matches. Then, as death takes over, the scene widens briefly to show the dead man and a greater, rejoicing nature.

Characters

The key to the story is the character of the nameless Everyman. London tells us that "The trouble with him was that he was without imagination." (p. 204) Also, "He was not given much to thinking ..." (p. 205). The students should see at once that the man's observations, careful scheduling, and confidence will be negated by a lack of experience and the inability to see the possible consequences of events.

Frequently students miss the many changes that take place within the man as he reacts to immediate happenings. London gives us the following moods and reactions:

1. The man "celebrates," because he is on schedule. (p. 206)

2. He is "a bit frightened," as his extremities become numb. (p. 208)
3. The man is "angry," when he falls into the water. (p. 209)
4. He is "keenly aware of his danger," as his feet begin to freeze. (p. 210)
5. "He was safe," with the fires started. (p. 211)
6. "The man was shocked," after the snow had smothered his fire. (p. 212)
7. ". . . he thought in the moment of controlled despair that ensued," as the wires between mind and body come down. (p. 213)
8. "A certain fear of death, dull and oppressive, came to him," when he realizes that he is physically incapable of killing the dog. (p. 216)
9. "He ran blindly, without intention, in fear such as he never had known in his life," as he struggles vainly to stay alive. (p. 216)
10. Resigned to his death, he gives in, "Well, he was bound to freeze anyway, and he might as well take it decently." (p. 217)

The dog, on the other hand, is a creature of nature and its instincts provide for its survival. London contrasts the dog with the man by clearly pointing out, "Its instincts told it a truer tale than was told to the man by the man's judgment." (p. 205)

Setting

London uses the setting as the third character in the story and also to create tone. It is a relentless adversary, a palpable force that never abates and finally drives the man into making his mistake. London sets the mood in the first two paragraphs of the story. In the first, the repetition of the adjectives "cold and gray" along with the verb "broken" immediately set a challenge. He follows these with the use of "intangible pall," "a subtle gloom," and the repeated comment that there was no sun. This paragraph should be contrasted with the last. After the man dies, nature seems to celebrate when, "A little longer it [the dog] delayed, howling under the stars that leaped and danced and shone brightly in the sky." (p. 218) The active, almost human role played by nature is seen in its duplicity for, "At a place where there were no signs, where the soft, unbroken snow seemed to advertise solidity beneath, the man broke through." (p. 209) Later, nature waits until the man has succeeded in building a fire and then calmly puts it out.

Tone

London gives the reader an uneasy feeling as he becomes an eyewitness to death. This is accomplished by the coupling of vivid pictures and an appeal to the reader's senses. Throughout the story London creates memorable pictures:

1. the frozen spit (p. 204)
2. the frozen muzzle of tobacco juice (p. 205)
3. the man's freezing hands (p. 208)
4. the lifeless fingers (p. 211).

London constantly appeals to our senses in the story, particularly in the following:

1. the description of the biscuits (p. 204)
2. the slow numbing of the man's body (pp. 212-13)
3. the burning flesh (p. 214)

Questions
1. What traits does the man possess?
2. Why is he unnamed?
3. What is London saying about man and nature?
4. In what ways are the first two paragraphs important?
5. How does the setting reflect London's basic theme?
6. What is naturalism? How does it appear in this story?

"The Lottery" by Shirley Jackson

Source: *50 Great Short Stories* edited by Milton Crane
Recommended level: senior/junior high school

Content—Discussing Theme

A provocative and often unsettling short story, "The Lottery" will engender a great deal of discussion. Not strong in plot, characterization, or setting, the story idea is both fascinating and terrifying. The work cannot be subjected to a simple theme statement for it involves no clear-cut conflict, but rather a painful awareness of man's past and the archetypal fears that appear in what Carl Jung refers to as the "collective unconscious."

The students will see the shock value of the story. A contemporary, small-town group of people meet in the town square (highly suggestive of early New England democracy at work) on a beautiful day for the annual lottery. Here the "winner" is immediately stoned to death and the rest of the townsfolk return to normal, daily activities. Played against the backdrop of a typical, friendly, all-American town, the action becomes inexplicable in terms of motivation and objective.

If the students are unable to fathom the apparently amoral attitude of the townsfolk, the instructor will have to take them back to man's earliest days and his primeval fears. Undoubtedly, Shirley Jackson is portraying these fears in a contemporary setting, bridging the moral gap between neolithic and modern man. The ritual of sacrifice has been with man from very early times. In pre-Greek matrilineal societies, which tended to be agricultural, the ruling queen's handpicked male consort was killed at the end of a year's tenure, his blood and body scattered over the fields to ensure the ground's fertility. This practice was by no means localized nor relegated to a particular people. Joseph Campbell (*The Masks of God: Occidental Mythology,* New York: The Viking Press, 1971, p. 147) says, "The leading mythological theme throughout the tropical, equatorial zone is of the killed and cut-up divine being out of whose body the food plants grew." Eventually, the queen spared the king and a king-substitute, usually a young man, was sacrificed. Finally, after the matrilineal structure was replaced by the patrilineal, a carved image of the king was ritually buried in the ground to convey the king's strength and fertility to the soil. It is to these dark beginnings that Shirley Jackson returns. Old Man Warner bemoans the young people in the other towns giving up their lotteries. He angrily says, " 'First thing you know, we'd all be eating stewed chickweed and acorns.' " (p. 135) Without a sacrifice, the crops will not grow. In this work Shirley Jackson has investigated in a modern setting the deeper meanings of ritual sacrifice, man's fears, and the sharing of communal guilt.

Form—Elements of the Story

Plot

The story is fast-paced and matter-of-fact. Suspense builds because the reader does not know the reward for winning the lottery. The careful reader will pick up signs of underlying fear (the people stay away from the box and the stool and become irritated by Mr. Summers' meaningless banter). However, once the traditional black spot is revealed, the story races to its conclusion. The pace of the narrative and the seemingly harmless statements about everyday life build the underlying tension and sense of horror.

Characters

There is little individual characterization; we are aware only of the group. It meets. It selects the lots. It acts. The author uses the characters, however, to throw the reader off at the beginning, heightening the impact of the story. They are everyday folks, concerned about "planting and rain, tractors and taxes." (p. 131) The women hope to be finished in time for lunch. Everyone is eager to participate.

The horror, which lurks just beneath the surface of the story, comes out in the pathetic outcry of Tessie Hutchinson after she has "won" the lottery. Tessie's repeated cry is, " 'It wasn't fair.' " (p. 136) She is only worried about the procedural aspects of the lottery; the moral aspects are not questioned.

Setting

In a second reading of the story, the students should see how Jackson has cleverly given clues to the meaning of the ritual. The first sentence makes us aware of the purpose—to ensure the fertility and profundity of nature:

The morning of June 27th was *clear* and *sunny*, with the *fresh warmth* of a *full-summer* day; the flowers were *blossoming profusely* and the grass was *richly green*. (this author's italics)

On page 131 the stones are mentioned four times and, purposely, the author has associated them with the children and children's games. Setting is used to bring out the irony found in the story, and with its close contact to the nature of the ritual, heighten the feeling of horror.

Tone

Shirley Jackson has used a matter-of-fact narrative which focuses throughout on happy children in contrast with a sinister act to create a story that startles the reader into realizing the underlying, irrational horror of life. This is gained by the "surprise" ending which completes the irony found throughout the work in the title, the setting, the characters, and the action. In addition, shock is created when many of the lines are re-read and the reader sees not only the seeds of ritual murder, but the complete acceptance of a necessary fact of life. Several examples of this include:

1. ". . . the whole lottery took less than two hours, so it could begin at ten o'clock in the morning and still be through in time to allow the villagers to get home for noon dinner." (p. 131)
2. "The lottery was conducted—as were the square dances, the teenage club, the Halloween program—by Mr. Summers, who had time and energy to devote to civic activities." (p. 131)
3. "The children had stones already, and someone gave little Davy Hutchinson a few pebbles." (p. 138)

Questions

1. What is the central action of the story?
2. Why do these people act this way every year?
3. Where else, when, and for what reasons has this occurred in man's history?
4. What role is played by Old Man Warner?
5. Upon re-reading the story, what examples of irony can be found?
6. How does the story relate to man's coping with his serious problems?

"The Catbird Seat" by James Thurber

Source: *50 Great Short Stories* edited by Milton Crane
Recommended level: senior/junior high school

Content—Discussing Theme

Thurber returns once again to one of his favorite themes
—the battle between the sexes—but this story is different.
His familiar adversaries wage the war—the dominant, loud,
voracious female and the quiet, timid, clumsy, submissive
male—but this time the weaker male triumphs. Ironically,
and typical of Thurber's approach to humor through the
unexpected, Mr. Martin triumphs at the moment of despair
when he realizes he cannot go through with his plan to "rub
out" Mrs. Barrows.

Unlike Walter Mitty or Mr. Preble, Mr. Martin is alert
enough to see that his careful preparations, along with his reputation, are enough to carry out a grand deception. The un-
planned stroke of genius comes to him like a transcendental
insight ("It was more than that; it was impossible." p. 327)
Knowing himself, Mr. Fitweiler, and his associates, Mr. Martin leaves Mrs. Barrows' apartment assured of his coming
victory. His parting remark to his mortal enemy, " 'I'm sitting in the catbird seat,' " is his final tribute to a frightening
opponent. Mr. Martin manages to cope with his problem and
Thurber is at his best in showing us the victory.

Form—Elements of the Story

Plot

Beginning the story *in medias res* (in the middle), Thurber
provides an element of suspense by introducing us to Mr.
Martin in the opening paragraph and showing us his unusual
behavior. By using a flashback and the third person limited
point of view, from Mr. Martin's viewpoint, however, the author states the conflict quickly and unfolds the battle at a
rapid pace. Instead of building up to the climax, where Mr.
Martin is forced to make a crucial decision, Thurber has Mr.
Martin fall into the solution abetted by a blunt knife, a high-
ball, and the unsuspecting Mrs. Barrows.

Characters

In the persons of Mr. Martin (note the absence of an informal first name) and Mrs. Barrows (her first name, Ulgine, is a bit ugly sounding) we see the ultimate in character contrast.

Martin is just what we would expect from an orderly, mild-mannered, impeccable, milk-drinking file clerk. To him, "rub out" has a quaint accounting sound to it. Mr. Martin's actions and thoughts are dominated by his passion for precision and order:

1. He eats on schedule at Schraffts (a place usually associated with elderly women stopping in for sweets after a show).
2. He builds his plan to get rid of Mrs. Barrows carefully and presents the need for it in the form of a mock trial, delivered alone at home over a glass of milk.
3. As Martin proceeds to Mrs. Barrows' apartment, through his eye view the reader becomes painfully aware of numbers (". . . eighteen minutes after nine . . ." "Twelfth Street," ". . . no one within fifty paces . . ." p. 326).

The contrast within Martin provides the humor as we see his carefully orchestrated plans and then notice his singular inability to carry them out:

1. He simply does not know how to kill; he expects to find a murder weapon lying about conveniently.
2. In the apartment, he suddenly becomes aware that Mrs. Barrows was ". . . larger than he had thought." (p. 326)
3. His clumsiness made any physical act almost impossible.

At the very end, with Mrs. Barrows' fate resolved and his department saved, Martin triumphantly and slowly returns to the safety of his files.

Mrs. Ulgine Barrows is best characterized by the verbs used to point out her actions and her speeches. Throughout the story the reader can find the following: "profaned," "romped," "brayed," "demanded," "bawled," "catapulted," and "screamed." These help bring out the dominant physical presence of this loud-voiced, slang-slinging, power-hungry woman.

Setting

Martin's timidity and sense of order are accentuated by his position in the filing department, the very nature of F & S, the mention of Schraffts, and the careful noting of specific street names and numbers. While the story "could take place anywhere," these details work to build the necessary character of Mr. Martin.

Tone

The humor of the story is built upon the familiar contrast between what a man is and what he would like to be. The scene where he enters Mrs. Barrows' apartment, with his sudden fear of the "monstrously bright" hallway ceiling light and the fear that he might cough too loud from the cigarettes, creates a picture of the absurd Mr. Martin. The picture continues to grow, and the mood becomes more ridiculous as he moves down the hall swiftly on tiptoe, shoves Mrs. Barrows into her room, and then proceeds to knock over items while he looks in vain for a murder weapon.

Thurber's style is used to recreate the emotional state of Mr. Martin. During the mock trial scene in his apartment, the sentences tend to be balanced, orderly, and quite logical. They move cleanly from point to point, and examples are freely given. (p. 323) However, in Mrs. Barrows' apartment, Martin's frantic search and growing agitation are recorded by Thurber in a series of short, subject-verb-object sentences that come one after another in a shotgun effect. Later, with Mr. Martin's victory assured, Thurber returns to the longer, slower-reading complex sentence.

The students must be reminded that often the surface reading of a Thurber story can be misleading, for the humor is found in his careful use of the right word and the juxtaposition of what is and what should be.

Questions
1. In what way is the title ironic?
2. How does Thurber make use of contrasts in the story?
3. In what way is the point of view expressed important to the story?
4. In what ways are Thurber's choice of words and style of writing important?

"The Archimandrite's Niece"
by James Reid Parker

Source: *50 Great American Short Stories* edited by Milton Crane

Recommended level: senior high school

Content—Discussing Theme

In this entertaining character sketch, Parker presents us with a character who finds it difficult, if not impossible, to cope with others, especially those who possess diametrically opposed personalities.

The purpose of the work is to portray a man so stiff and so colorless that he is unable to perceive the motives of others. Dedicated to his job and the preservation of order in his bachelorhood, Mr. Devore (note the absence of a familiar first name) cannot conceive of the amorous intentions of Mrs. Kraft to find him a suitable wife, although this has presumably happened before (" 'I'm always picking out the perfect wife for you, Henry,' " she said, " 'and you never give them the least little bit of encouragement.' " p. 415).

As the students read the surprising last sentence and picture Mrs. Kraft's intent, they should go back to the confrontation of the two people most unlike each other in almost every respect.

Form—Elements of the Story

Characters

Through his comments, his surroundings, and his reactions to Mme. Liapchev, Mr. Devore is revealed to be a man who is:

1. colorless and unemotional
2. motivated solely by business concerns
3. unimaginative
4. dedicated to order and the rational explanation of life ("The beauty of the law ... was the beauty of its codified orderliness." p. 409).

Mr. Devore knows that he spoke on the phone with Mrs. Kraft about Mme. Liapchev for 23 minutes, but he never reads into Mrs. Kraft's comment when she introduces her friend as "A charming person . . . and one whom Mr. Devore was sure to admire and pity." (p. 409) Later on, during a lull in Mme. Liapchev's lively assault on Mr. Devore's ears, "—she became gentle once more, and there was an alarmingly intimate quality in her voice when she was gentle—" (p. 413), but by this time Mr. Devore is too upset to realize anything, except that he has to get this woman out of his office and his life.

Mme. Liapchev is a moving force quite unlike Mr. Devore. She is attractive, outgoing, expressive (note how she reacts immediately to his futile comments), and loquacious. In her liveliness, she loves to shock her listener with outrageous comments such as " 'God will wash and refresh your soul!' " (p. 410) As she speaks forth with a "musical quaver" in her voice, she is equally unaware that she is offending Devore by destroying all semblance of order in their "discussion." He is ignorant of names, places, and events, and can do nothing in the situation (if it actually exists) because he can make little sense out of it. Thus, completely frustrated and antagonized by a force he cannot comprehend, Devore shows Mme. Liapchev out of his office and attempts to replace chaos with order.

Setting

The drab, colorless office, hardly more cheerful than the "sulphur-yellow splotches in the gray waste" outside his windows, reinforces the attributes given to the main character. Mr. Devore's office is one of "austerity" and is called a "temple" by his sister.

Tone

The humor of the story comes through the ill-fated confrontation between two very dissimilar personalities. Parker also catches the stiffness and formality of Mr. Devore in his impressive but vague title and in the structure of his opening sentences. Note the stilted, awkward, unemotional tone of the following:

He would have denied at any time, but particularly on this

dreary morning, that his professional life was informed with color, and would have insisted that this was not a matter for regret. (p. 409)

Questions
1. What does the title do for the story?
2. In what ways is the character of Mr. Devore revealed?
3. Is Mme. Liapchev genuine? Why, or why not?
4. What happens to Devore during his interview with Mme. Liapchev?
5. What does the ending reveal about Devore?
6. How is the style of the story effective?

"The Bride Comes to Yellow Sky"
by Stephen Crane

Source: *50 Great American Short Stories* edited by Milton Crane
Recommended level: senior high school

Content—Discussing Theme

When students quickly read Crane's "The Bride Comes to Yellow Sky," they often go no further than the surface plot and see little in the story. The buildup to the actionless confrontation disappoints the careless reader who expects to find the equivalent of a grade-B western. When asked for the theme, many students will struggle to establish a meaningful statement for what seems to be a puzzling story.

Here then, is a good story to demonstrate that sometimes a writer's purpose outweighs his dramatic theme statement. In the two main characters we have two men coping with problems. Sheriff Jack Potter must cope with his fear of returning to Yellow Sky with a bride and suffering the reaction of the townspeople. The reaction of the town is limited to Scratchy

Wilson, who must now cope with a threat to his lifestyle—Potter's new bride.

Beyond the main characters, though, Crane is having fun with his short story. The handling of the elements reveals that the author is satirizing the local color western by presenting a work rich in contrasts. These contrasts, and the resulting humor, are heightened by his use of the mock-heroic style. Since satire is sometimes difficult for students to understand, the teacher can help by using leading questions and filling in the necessary background.

Form—Elements of the Story

Plot

Crane uses plot to tell a straightforward story in which action and mood steadily build up to the unexpected ending. The story is divided into four parts which could be titled as follows: (encourage students to form their own titles)

Part I: The Fear of Return
Part II: The Fear of Scratchy
Part III: Scratchy's Challenge
Part IV: The Confrontation

The students must remember that the familiar clichés and western stereotypes have been built by countless stories and western movies that came after Crane wrote this work. Nevertheless, Crane's plot is filled with contrasts that constantly provide the reader with humor. For example:

1. the dignity of the coach vs. the coarseness of Potter and his bride
2. the joy of the couple vs. Potter's dread of having to face the citizens of Yellow Sky
3. the "ferocity" of Scratchy vs. the quiet of the town

The story does not conform to the ideal plot line because the basic conflict of the work is not the same for both major characters. On the surface, and for Scratchy, the conflict rests in the ultimate, and oft-repeated, showdown and shootout, while for Potter, even the face-to-face meeting with Scratchy is secondary to being caught on the street with his new bride before he can reach the safety of his home.

Characters

It should be obvious to the careful reader that contrasts abound in the characters of both Jack and Scratchy. From the barkeeper's comments, to the drummer's reactions, the reader can feel the strength of Jack Potter (even his name reminds us of the field where many have been sent after death). It is there below the surface in the plush railroad car. However, it is not his forcefulness and strength we see in the story, but rather the overpowering shyness and awkwardness of a man afraid of being seen with his wife.

Scratchy's contrasts are even more noticeable and amusing. His reputation in Part II is a strong one and the reactions to his arrival indicate a ferocity seldom matched, except by the steadfast Sheriff. However, a look at Scratchy reveals quite a different person. His nickname suggests not a cold-blooded killer, but rather a pesty annoyance, and when he's sober, says the barkeeper, he " 'wouldn't hurt a fly ...' " (p. 146) Scratchy's apparel also belies his awesome reputation. Instead of wearing rugged, masculine western clothes that might seem strange to Easterners, Scratchy wears a maroon shirt made in New York City and favors red boots with gold designs that are favorites with New England children in the winter. Indeed, these observations, plus the heartbroken acceptance of Potter's withdrawal from their periodic ritual, reveal only a softhearted old drunk.

Setting

Crane appears to give us the "typical" western filled with all the local color needed to engross the reader. There are typical characters (barkeeper, drummer, "killer," strong sheriff) and the quintessential shootout. It is just these elements that Crane uses to satirize and play with as he presents a far from typical western.

Tone

Crane's delight in the story comes through in many humorous touches that can be found throughout the work. Among the many "western" characteristics that are contrasted are the following:

1. The "lady" is not the typical young schoolmarm but rather a homely, shy cook.
2. The strong, leathery, rugged individualist is a shy, gangling, embarrassed husband.
3. Scratchy tacks up a piece of paper on the saloon door but misses it in practice.
4. Instead of a deadly shootout there is an awkward, embarrassing bump-in.

In addition, Crane creates a humorous takeoff on physical courage and the deadly confrontation between giants of men by using a mock-heroic approach to the story. Throughout the work there are humorous comparisons to the ancient Homeric epics and the valiant contests between famous warriors. Students may not be familiar with the form of the epic so the teacher may have to bring out the following or have a student look up and list epic qualities:

1. the use of the Homeric simile
   a. ". . . wood that gleamed as darkly brilliant as the surface of a pool of oil." (p. 140)
   b. ". . . the shadow of a deed weigh upon him like a leaden slab." (p. 141)
   c. ". . . her face had gone as yellow as old cloth." (p. 148)
2. the use of the heroic epithet
   a. the barkeeper referred to as "the man of bottles" (p. 146)
   b. Scratchy referred to as "He of the revolver" (p. 148)
3. As Aeneas flees burning Troy, hiding from marauding Greeks, so Potter and his wife sneak into town, hiding from the eyes of the townspeople.
4. As heroes before Troy uttered challenges to each other before individual combat, so Scratchy screams at Potter's empty house.
5. Crane repeatedly uses the number three, found often in mythology and in Homer:
   a. there are three Texans at the bar (p. 143)

b. Scratchy tries three times to break down the bar-room door (p. 145)

c. three gestures are made at the barkeeper (p. 145)

d. three wild cries of challenge ring out (p. 146)

e. three paces separate the two men (p. 148)

It is obviously Crane's intention to contrast the heroic past with the ignoble present, and the many comparisons and contrasts create a humorous picture of the "Old West."

Questions

1. Why is the story divided into four parts?
2. What kind of man is Potter? What is his wife like?
3. What use is made of description in Part I?
4. How is Scratchy revealed to the reader? What is he like?
5. Is there any conflict between Scratchy's reputation and his deeds? What are they?
6. In what ways is this a "typical" western?
7. What has happened to each man at the end?
8. Why is the title a good one, or isn't it?

"Mr. Preble Gets Rid of His Wife"

by James Thurber

Source: *50 Great American Short Stories* edited by Milton Crane

Recommended level: senior/junior high school

Content—Discussing Theme

The delightful stories of James Thurber amuse almost all readers. Seemingly simple stories on the surface, the works reveal a careful development and interrelationship of character, setting, and dialogue.

Like so many of his works, "Mr. Preble Gets Rid of His Wife" has been written to entertain. It continues Thurber's major theme of the battle between man and woman, in which he pits a dominant, devouring woman against an ineffective, bumbling, fantasizing male. In trying to cope with his wife

Mr. Preble begins a series of incongruities that lead the reader to laughter and delight.

Form—Elements of the Story

Plot

Like Mr. Preble, Thurber's plot line is simple, direct, businesslike—and not really a plot at all. Mr. Preble decides to leave his wife and discovers that he must get rid of her in order to run off with his secretary. After supper he attempts to lure Mrs. Preble into the cellar where the deed will be done. Following Mrs. Preble's suggestion to find a murder weapon outside the house, he leaves and, it seems, the affair is closed for the moment. He will probably stop at the cigar store and will not find the convenient murder weapon lying about.

Characters

Like Mr. Martin ("The Catbird Seat") and Walter Mitty ("The Secret Life of Walter Mitty"), Mr. Preble is a humorous incongruity. The contrast between the man and the act he wishes to commit is beautifully controlled by Thurber. Mr. Preble never says "murder" but rather "get rid of." He has no idea of how to commit such an act and will simply carry it out in the cellar where, he supposes, such things are done. Instead of being a cool, calculating deceiver, he is a plump, unemotional, stiff lawyer. Rebuffed by his wife, he can only kick at the rug or jingle his keys when his secretary amusingly agrees to go away with him. Exasperated by his wife's stubborn refusal to go downstairs to be killed, all Preble can muster is a "Gee whiz!" Even as he leaves the house to search somewhere for a murder weapon, the screams of his wife ring in his ears.

Mrs. Preble, like so many of Thurber's women, is a termagant. She is a tyrant and she knows her husband. She treats him like a child (" 'What's come over you?' " p. 266). She can read his face the way a mother can see through her child. Preble's announcement of his plans and his love for the secretary are met with an amused disdain, " 'We've been all over that, I'm not going to go all over that again.' " (p. 266) Undoubtedly, this scene has been played before with similar results. To quiet him down, let him work his fantasy out, and get him out of the house, Mrs. Preble reluctantly agrees to accompany Mr. Preble to the basement. Mrs. Preble was, and always will be, two steps ahead of her milquetoast husband.

Setting

Interestingly, the story takes place on a Monday. Was Preble's sudden proposal to his secretary and immediate acceptance of the need to kill his wife the familiar reaction to a long weekend at home?

Tone

The humor in the story begins with the straightforward, rather blunt title. Its meaning becomes more ironic as we meet Preble and his wife. The humor continues through the short work as Thurber builds incongruous situations and adds absurd dialogue.

The incongruities that abound in the story include the following:

1. Preble's character as opposed to the deed,
2. His wife's annoyed, condescending reaction to the proposal,
3. The secretary's careless, lighthearted reaction to Preble, and his interpretation of her acceptance,
4. Preble's annoyance at his wife's poor attitude to being murdered and buried in the cold cellar.

Students should be encouraged to read other Thurber stories and look for the humor found in absurd situations, witty dialogue, and ironic contrasts.

Questions

1. What kind of person is Mr. Preble?
2. How is his wife different?
3. What contrasts exist in the story?
4. How does the dialogue add to the overall effect of the story?
5. How, in your own words, does the story end? Why doesn't Thurber end it?
6. Why did Thurber word the title the way he did?

"A Man of the World" by Ernest Hemingway

Source: *50 Great American Short Stories* edited by Milton Crane

Recommended level: senior high school

Content—Discussing Theme

In this difficult but typical Hemingway short story, the reader is drawn quickly into the Hemingway world. Without a knowledge of this world gained from a reading of Hemingway's key stories, the young reader will find the story confusing. For many young readers, "A Man of the World" will be nothing more than a gruesome character sketch of a particularly loathsome character. They will come to realize that Blindy is proud of his deformity and that he has "earned" it. However, the question the young reader will ask is: what is there to be proud of?

Through student reading of other Hemingway short works along with oral reports to the class and key questions from the teacher, the class should be able to put together a picture of the interesting, but narrow Hemingway world. They should also see the excellent but limited pantheon of Hemingway characters. For Hemingway, the world is a cruel, hostile, indifferent place where man must relentlessly prove himself. One proves himself by living up to what has become called the "Hemingway Code." It demands from the individual an awareness of, and resignation to, death; honesty of action and emotion; a rejection of false values; a commitment to perfection in whatever one does; a scorning of sloppiness; and an appreciation of the simple, physical realities of life. Whether or not a character has been able to discover the "truth" about life will determine if he is among the "initiated" or the "uninitiated." A long list of Hemingway initiates would include the older waiter in "A Clean, Well-Lighted Place," the gambler in "The Nun, the Gambler, and the Radio," Wilson in "The Short Happy Life of Francis Macomber," and Santiago from "The Old Man and the Sea." Nick Adams, in many of the early Hemingway stories, is a good example of the uninitiated, as is the young waiter in "A Clean, Well-Lighted Place."

Blindy, a panhandling, offensive drunk, has lived violently, been cruelly maimed physically, but has continued on without giving in. Although not as noble as the Major in "In Another Country" or professionally skilled and morally attractive as Wilson in "The Short Happy Life of Francis Macomber," Blindy has made his own way. In some ways, he exhibits elements of the code hero:

1. He has developed an expertise—"The Blind man knew the sounds of all the different machines in the saloon." (p. 308)
2. He has a fierce pride—" 'Blindy's the name, Tom. I earned that name. You seen me earn it.' " (p. 311)
3. He is not defeated—" 'You know that Willie Sawyer he'll never be a man of the world.' " (p. 311)
4. He is not sloppy—"His hand reached out and found the glass and he raised it accurately to the three of us." (p. 312)

Like the newcomer in the bar, the reader is put in the role of the uninitiated. In the space of an hour or so, in a lonely bar in the midst of no place, he comes to see one man's view of life and the cost of not giving in to it.

Form—Elements of the Story

Plot

Like so many of Hemingway's stories, the work is basically plotless. The conflict has been resolved and the reader must fill in the facts, assess the character, and draw his own conclusions. In reading Hemingway, the younger reader must be aware of his use of understatement, the fuller meaning that lies between the lines, and not be swayed away from Hemingway's real world by the specific, violent action.

Characters

In this work the student should see the characters used repeatedly by Hemingway. These include:

1. the initiated (code hero)—sometimes called *the tutor*
2. the uninitiated (often a youth)—sometimes called *the tyro*
3. the impartial observer or narrator.

Setting

As in many of Hemingway's works, this one contains familiar aspects of setting. Hemingway tends to reduce the world to a very limited arena, or microcosm. This may be a lighted, warm bar or cafe in the midst of the cold, impersonal darkness. Quite often, the only comfort left to the initiated to escape the *nada* or nothingness of existence is the light, a drink, and for Blindy, the sounds of the slot machines along with the faithful accounting of the crippling fight with Willie Sawyer.

Tone

While many will find the details of the fight objectionable and shudder at the explicitness of the description, others will find that Hemingway's style creates in the reader a ready acceptance of the grotesque. This is accomplished by many typical Hemingway stylistic techniques which include the following:

1. A simple sentence structure emphasizing the subject-verb-object pattern. This brings a disarming simplicity to the tale.
2. The use of repetition. The constant reference to Blindy's blindness (five times in the first 16 sentences) and his offensive smell (note that Willie Sawyer probably never noticed this, to Blindy's delight) offset the disquieting pride that he has gained.
3. Dialogue that is deceptively simple and tends to lull the reader from Blindy's battle.

All these elements of Hemingway's style heighten the effect of Blindy's gloating over what he has done to Willie Sawyer, and the seeming cruelty of Hemingway's world. Blindy gleefully asserts, " 'Did it again [felt Willie Sawyer's face] tonight too . . . That's why he put me out of the car. He ain't got no sense of humor at all . . . he'll never be a man of the world.' " (p. 311)

Questions
1. What kind of a person is Blindy?
2. What had happened to him? Why?
3. Why is so much time spent on the setting?
4. How is the point of view helpful to the story?
5. What, according to the story, is "a man of the world"?

"Silent Snow, Secret Snow" by Conrad Aiken

Source: *50 Great American Short Stories* edited by Milton Crane

Recommended level: senior high school

Content—Discussing Theme

In this fine short story dealing with the inability of a young 12-year-old boy to cope with his surroundings and eventually himself, Aiken gives us a sketch of a young man succumbing to a breakdown.

Paul Hasleman, a very bright, observant, sensitive young boy, has been underwhelmed by day-to-day existence and the routines of life. To compensate for his observations of the dreariness, the dirt, and the growing anxieties of Mother and Father, Paul retreats into his mind and conjures up the protective, insulating softness of snow. This submission to the unreal, to the security of rejection, and to the numbing, destructive forces of withdrawal finally brings him to the ultimate break with adults and to a total dependence upon his self-destructive dreams.

Form—Elements of the Story

Plot

Divided into four parts, the story portrays the rapid dissolution of Paul Hasleman's grasp on reality. These four sections seem to present the following decline:

I: A way to escape
II: The ugliness of reality
III: The examination
IV: The escape to unreality

Since each episode accounts for a specific experience, although they culminate in the final break in Section IV, the plot line will not follow the ideal line; this happens in many character-centered stories.

Technically the students should be aware of the flashback in Part I, when time is suspended during the geography lesson and Paul daydreams about the beginning of his obsession. The need for the third person omniscient author should be seen as we get an idea of Paul's two worlds.

Characters

Although a character sketch, the story does not give us a complete picture of young Paul. Aiken focuses on Paul's obsession and this is how we see the boy. The world is seen through Paul's eyes, and he screens out all but the unpleasant. Also, Paul focuses on the unseen postman as the most important person in his life. As Paul realizes that he might have missed the symbolic postman, who might tell Paul that he has achieved the moment of slipping away from the ugly, real world into the beautiful, unreal one, he thinks, "Did it mean ... that he would never hear the postman again?—that tomorrow morning the postman would already have passed the house, in a snow by then so deep as to render his footsteps completely inaudible ... A vague feeling of disappointment came over him, a vague sadness, as if he felt himself deprived of something which he had long looked forward to, something much prized." (p. 242)

Although never named so that they become live, warm people, Paul's parents remain Mother and Father throughout the story. They are simply forces hostile to Paul's growing aloofness. The students should note that he does not react to them, but rather to the tones of their voices. They are depersonalized by him just as his own personality is being consumed by the breakdown.

Setting

The setting throughout the story is one that relates closely to Paul's frame of mind. In Part I, during the geography lesson, the sight of the Poles sets him daydreaming although Miss Buell is discussing the Equator. The warm sunny days at home become snow-filled days in his mind. In Part II, the dismal picture of the walk home is seen through Paul's eyes. He magnifies the ugliness (his snow world is a place of "ethereal loveliness") and Aiken saturates the page with sordid images and ugly words—"black," "dessicated," "dull in color as dead fruit left in leafless trees," "delta of filth," "dead matches." (pp. 238-9) Even the birds have left the little bird-house in the apple tree (p. 240) just as Paul is planning "to leave" his own house. In Part III, as Paul is being questioned by the doctor and his parents, he looks beyond them to the fire where "the fingers of flame [were] making light prestidigitation against the sooty fireback, the soft sound of the random flutter [was] the only sound." (p. 244) This sound was similar to the soothing, soft, sensuous sound of the snow. In Part IV, Paul's room has become his shrinking cell, the mind within which he can withdraw from the real world to the comfort and warmth provided by the sound-enveloping snow.

Tone

Aiken makes excellent use of his description to convey Paul's thoughts and outlook. Particularly the snow scenes, with the repeated use of sibilants, alliteration, and participles, create a mood of serenity. Coupled with the image of the in-ward-growing flower and the diminution of all sounds and senses, these scenes convey the extreme world into which Paul is rapidly and smoothly falling. The joy felt by Paul, and conveyed through these scenes, puts a chill into the perceptive reader who sees the path of destruction that Paul has chosen.

Questions

1. Why does Aiken use this title?
2. What do we know, and not know, about Paul?
3. What is the view of the real world that we get in the story? Whose view is it?
4. In what ways are the other characters used?
5. What use is made of the diction, or choice of words, in the story?

"The Old People" by William Faulkner

Source: *50 Great American Short Stories* edited by Milton Crane
Recommended level: senior high school

Content—Discussing Theme

Faulkner poses problems for most readers, and for high

school readers he can confuse and frustrate even the good student. Excerpts from his rambling novels, often anthologized as short stories, are incomprehensible while many short stories seem to be puzzling in plot and filled with eccentric, strange characters. Faulkner's Ciceronian sentences, his annoying habit of interweaving characters from novel to story (which presumes that the reader knows them), and his use of indefinite pronoun references that invite interpretation rather than mere close reading, all tend to baffle the reader not familiar with Faulkner and Yonapatawphy County.

Despite the difficulties, the teacher should not miss the opportunity to have the students attempt a work by one of America's finest writers and Nobel Prize winners. In this work, outwardly dealing with a young boy's coping with a problem of growing up and being accepted by his elders, Faulkner presents an even deeper concern for the major themes and motifs that run through his works:

1. the towering, mute presence of the wilderness—*the land,*
2. the nobility and endurance of early races, particularly the Indian (early rulers) and to some extent the Negro (the symbol of endurance through bondage and servility)—*the people,*
3. the problems of the heart—*the soul.*

These themes are subtly worked into the central theme of the initiation of Ike (Isaac) McCaslin into:
1. the world of the hunter
2. the worlds of life and death
3. the world of love and common kinship.

Form—Elements of the Story

Plot

Once the students have become acquainted with the length and complexity of the Faulknerian sentence (hopefully with the guidance of the teacher, before their own reading), a study of the plot line should be carefully made. The story, a relatively simple one, follows the motif of the quest.

Part I: 1. Opens with Ike killing his first deer at age 12.

2. Homage is paid to Sam Fathers in a long flash-back that covers Ike's remembrance of Sam from the age of 7 on. The flashback, narrated mostly by Ike's cousin, deals with:
   a. Sam's father, Ikemotubbe, and Sam's sale to the McCaslins (pp. 283-84).
   b. Sam's stubborn pride and independence (pp. 284-86).
   c. Sam's tutoring of Ike in hunting skills and in the history of "the old people" (pp. 286-87).

Part II: 1. The return to the present and the preparation for the trip back home.
2. The trip home is interrupted by the tracking of a large deer and the final shooting of a much smaller one.

Part III: The return home to Major de Spain's.

Like many of Faulkner's stories, this work does not build to a climax and then resolve the conflict. The climactic event—the killing of the deer and Ike's ceremonial baptism in the deer's warm blood—happens immediately, and then we get a long, discursive flashback that centers on Sam Fathers. However, Ike continues to learn as Faulkner presents a parallel scene, the stalking of the second deer, but Ike does not kill in this contrasting episode. Reminiscent of the realization that comes to Francis Macomber during the second hunt in Hemingway's "The Short Happy Life of Francis Macomber," Ike becomes aware of the need for life, not death, as Sam stretches forth his hand and chants his mysterious prayers of adoration to the passing deer, undoubtedly an animal representation (totem) of Sam's dead ancestors—the old people.

Characters

While one can spend time investigating the exotic gallery of Faulkner's oddities, this work basically deals with two characters—Sam Fathers (age) and Ike McCaslin (youth). In some ways the two are related:

1. Sam was sold into slavery by a father he never knew.

Ike's father was so old that the boy never really knew him.
2. Both are loners.
3. Sam is at the end of a line. Ike is at the beginning.

Sam Fathers, as his name indicates, is both the spiritual and acting father to young Ike. Their relationship follows an archetypal theme (the search for the missing father) very popular in today's fiction. A combination of fierce pride (as the son of a chief) and humility (as part Negro, Sam has inherited their pain of bondage and servility), Sam bridges the distance between past and present; he binds himself and young Ike to the land, and his teaching comes not only from experience but from deep within his heart, catching the spiritual needs of man for man and man for the land.

Young Ike McCaslin, the spiritual son of Sam to whom Sam entrusts his love of man, animal, and the land, learns more than he bargained for during the hunt. Merely seeking to become a hunter accepted by the veteran hunters and to be allowed to sit by the evening fire sharing in the time-worn stories, Ike comes to learn:

1. what *not* to kill ("... when to shoot and when not to shoot, when to kill and when not to kill, and better, what to do with it afterward" p. 286),
2. that there is more to life than telling old stories around a fire,
3. that we are inextricably bound to the past and to the land,
4. that being a hunter is not necessarily being a man.

Ike comes to see most of this in the second hunting scene in which the ritual of worship and respect contrasts with the earlier ritual of death. The scene is one of intimacy (Sam stands beside him—this is mentioned twice) and nobility (the deer passes by effortlessly with wild, full, unafraid eyes). After moaning about missing the deer, Ike, with lowered rifle, can only watch the deer go by and listen to Sam's chanting. The scene closes powerfully as the air is filled with the sound of Walter Ewell's horn blowing in empty triumph.

Setting

The woods serve as more than a locale in the story. At

times they become a *persona*, a force in the work that must be reckoned with. As described by Faulkner, the woods are almost human. Ike returns from a visit to the woods with

> . . . an unforgettable sense of the big woods—not a quality dangerous or particularly inimical, but profound, sentient, gigantic and brooding, amid which he had been permitted to go to and fro at will, unscathed, why he knew not, but dwarfed and, until he had drawn honorably blood worthy of being drawn, alien. (p. 290)

As the hunters make their way to the camp, the woods are again described as: ". . . stooping a little, watching them and listening, not quite inimical because they were too small . . . just brooding, secret, tremendous, almost inattentive." (p. 291) When Sam stops breathing during the hunt, the woods seem to cease all movement in spiritual camaraderie (p. 292). It is the wilderness, with the trees, the graceful deer and savage bear, and the spirits of the noble people of the past with which Ike has developed a kinship. It is this new feeling that he wants to keep when he answers his cousin McCaslin, " 'But we want them. . . . We want them too. There is plenty of room for us and them too.' " (p. 298)

Tone

The feeling of the distant past, of the mysterious creatures who peopled the earth before, and of the unspoken bond between age (the past) and youth (the present) pervades this story.

In the first hunting scene Sam stands behind the boy and mechanically tells him how to shoot, when to shoot, how to approach the downed deer, and how to draw the blood. The sentences, although long, have a repetitious subject-verb-object format. The repetition of "he" makes the paragraphs sound machine-like. The buck acts like a deer and its antlers look like a small rocking chair. However, the scene at the end is quite different. Sam says very little, and the boy feels he will remember everything. This is in contrast to the first scene where he would forget the moment he killed the buck. The deer in the second hunt scene acts very unlike a hunted deer. The "he" of the first scene becomes the "it" of the second. The deer is all important as a force and life, not death, is supreme.

The teacher can overcome the students' reticence caused

by Faulkner's difficult style and interest the student in reading more of the major works of this fine writer by picking out the strengths of the story and recommending other readable Faulkner works.

Questions
1. Why does Faulkner use this title?
2. What kind of person is Sam? Ike?
3. What does the setting add to the story?
4. How does McCaslin Edwards differ from Ike? Where do you see this?
5. In what ways are the two hunting scenes alike? Different?
6. What point of view does Faulkner use? Why?
7. In what ways does Ike change during the story? Why?

"Young Goodman Brown"
by Nathaniel Hawthorne

Source: *50 Great American Short Stories* edited by Milton Crane
Recommended level: senior high school

Content—Discussing Theme

"Young Goodman Brown" deals with Hawthorne's oft-repeated themes of sin and guilt. It is a tale of a man in conflict with himself. Brown—a good, young man—naively respects the many "good" people around him, wrestles with an inner urge that forces him to embark on a desperate journey into the woods at night. Even with the Puritan attitudes toward darkness and the forest as the dwelling places of evil, Brown is forced to go by his curiosity, the attraction of impending evil (p. 11), and by his naive outlook (" '. . . and after this one night I'll cling to her skirts and follow her to heaven.' " p. 7).

Brown atttempts to cope with his own problem of moral identity and to understand himself by initially hiding behind his "goodness" and his family's reputation. As he ventures further into the forest and as more is revealed to him about his neighbors by his satanic guide, Brown sees how easily his moral skin is punctured. He overhears mingled sounds along the roadside, and the murmur of voices floats down from a wind-driven cloud. In one "stupefied moment" Brown loses his belief, his past, and his faith as he madly careens through the forest to his appointed midnight communion service. Here, Hawthorne's favorite themes come into play as Goodman Brown finds himself unable to cope with what is happening, or what he thinks is happening. These themes include the following:

1. sin and its effects
2. the nature of guilt
3. the struggle between the heart (feeling, art) and the mind (reason, science)
4. the hardening of the heart
5. the sin of pride.

Coming to grips with the ubiquitous nature of evil as he gazes on the vague, barely distinguishable faces that ring the forest clearing, Brown rejects the multitude as sinful and clings desperately to his own goodness; his pride has rendered him unable to accept the presence of evil in every human being. His mind has turned his heart to stone. Like Ethan Brand, Almyer, Reverend Hooper, and Rappaccini, Goodman Brown has been unable to solve his problem and attain self-understanding. His inability to comprehend, as Hawthorne puts it, ". . . words which expressed all that our nature can conceive of sin, and darkly hinted at far more" (p. 15), leaves him as it does the other Hawthorne characters—alone, misunderstood and misunderstanding, and unable to feel.

Form—Elements of the Story

Plot

The basic plot line of the story is based on the universal, mythological quest tale (the search, the journey). Like many of the Greek heroes, Brown is mysteriously urged (the classic prophecy) to go on a journey of discovery. Along the way he meets a guide (usually divine help, in the classic tale) who takes him to the nether world of the dark forest. At the beginning of the work the use of foreshadowing (p. 7) builds suspense and brings out character.

Characters

Hawthorne makes use of characters so that they stand for ideas (allegory). In the tradition of the Medieval Everyman and Bunyan's searching Pilgrim, Goodman Brown, Faith, and the forest guide represent rungs on the moral ladder. Brown is a common, naive, unaware, simple, and curious man intrigued by the evil in his quest (pp. 7-8). Faith seems to know something. Her attempt to dissuade her husband from going and her exuberant welcome at his return show us the person who can balance the knowledge of evil (red) with love (white). Truly, her ribbons should be pink. Brown's mysterious guide, recognized by Goody Cloyse as the devil, is given a number of dark attributes. He moves like the wind, carries a black, snakelike staff, is seemingly ageless, uncannily resembles his young companion, and has a touch that withers (see the heartless Rappaccini in "Rappaccini's Daughter").

Hawthorne enjoys using symbols. In "Young Goodman Brown" his characters are built by the effective use of names and colors.

Setting

The setting, which is so vital to this story, adds a touch of irony to the work. Brown leaves the safety of the town for the dark, forbidding forest. However, although he searches for knowledge—the movement of the story goes from darkness (sunset-ignorance) to light (sunrise-awakening)—Brown goes from a benign ignorance to an unfeeling, destructive knowledge of mankind.

It is also the setting that holds Hawthorne's use of Romantic elements. Since the Romantic Movement (a good subject for student reports) involved the beneficial, almost sacred aspects of nature—the victory of emotion and feeling over reason, brooding heroes, and the use of bizarre and supernatural events—we can understand Hawthorne's use of the unexplainable.

Tone

The feelings of mystery, suspense, surprise, and the overtones of fantasy are brought out by Hawthorne's symbolic handling of characters and his use of Romantic description. The "unreal" feeling is brought out by the carefully developed possibility that the whole sequence of events never occurred. Even Brown asks if he was just dreaming the entire night. Except for the ever-present pink ribbons, isn't it possible that Brown had experienced in his own fears the moon-reflected leaves of trees, the rushing wind, the snapping twigs, and the rustling bushes that combined to create a Disney-like phantasmagoria?

Questions

1. In what ways is Goodman Brown unlike the others in the story both before and after his journey?
2. What does Hawthorne mean when he says, "... and there was a world of meaning in this simple comment"? (p. 10)
3. What is it that forces Brown to his meeting after he decides not to go?
4. What movements (changes) are found in the story?
5. In what ways do the characters represent ideas or attitudes?
6. What strength or weakness forces Brown to his final condition?
7. What is Hawthorne saying about the nature of man? Where does he specifically say this?
8. Where do we find the use of foreshadowing? What purpose does it serve?
9. How does Hawthorne use setting to achieve certain effects in the story?
10. What elements of Romanticism can be found in the story?

"For Esmé—With Love and Squalor"

by J. D. Salinger

Source: *50 Great Short Stories* edited by Milton Crane
Recommended level: senior high school

Content—Discussing Theme

J. D. Salinger's subtlety of purpose, his care in developing a story, and his concern for language make this a difficult story for most readers. The young reader, seeing no overt conflict, and being sidetracked by conversations that seem to go no place (e.g. the narrrator and Charles, Sergeant X and Clay), will not look deeply into the characters of the narrator and Esmé.

The basic theme of the story is one familiar to most Salinger readers—the need to love and the consequences of being unable to love another. The narrator of the story tries to cope with the loneliness and uncertainties of life brought about by war. Esmé steps into his life at a moment of extreme loneliness; she is charming and confusing but ennobling. The remembrance of their short talk together and of the beautiful character of this strange, mysteriously mature young girl restores the narrator's confidence and snaps him out of the bottomless despair of a breakdown.

Form—Elements of the Story

Plot

Students will have to concentrate on the dialogue in this story to carefully uncover the basic characteristics of Esmé and the narrrator. However, they must not overlook important incidents of plot that help bring out the theme or help reveal character. The interplay between Charles and the narrator about the silly riddle reveals that the superficially pessimistic, hardnosed narrator is indeed sensitive. He feels Charles' infantile chagrin and mentions the riddle at their parting to restore Charles' happiness. The rather long dialogue with Clay in the second part of the story confirms the narrator's breakdown in combat and reveals his bitter frustration at not being able to function physically or mentally.

The seemingly unimportant presence of the copy of Goebbel's book leads to the basic theme of the story as the distraught narrator replies to the girl's written comment, " 'Dear God, life is hell,' " with a quote from Dostoevski, " '... I maintain that it is the suffering of being unable to love.' " (p. 200)

By going back to the opening two paragraphs after the story is finished, the students should see in the narrator's matter-of-fact tone and somewhat sarcastic comments about his levelheaded wife and aging mother-in-law that his love and admiration are still with and for the young girl he will never see again.

Finally, the students should notice the narrator's switch to the third person in the second part. It becomes too difficult to describe the breakdown, and he steps out of the picture to look in.

Characters

The similarities and differences of the narrator and Esmé are subtly brought out. They share many characteristics and experiences:

1. They are both lonely.
2. They are both looking for love.
3. They are both sensitive.
4. They both tend to hide behind a protective mask (i.e. the narrator's detached, negative outlook and Esmé's blasé eyes).

The young narrator, just out of college and as of yet an unpublished short story writer, tends to be somewhat introverted (writes letters and reads by himself), pessimistic (he threw his gas mask out a porthole because he knew it wouldn't do any good), individualistic (he wears his hat in a unique style), sensitive, and quite skeptical (he doesn't seem to believe Esmé's title). He is also very lonely—to avoid Esmé's pointed questions he makes up a wife that doesn't exist.

Although he found the short encounter with Esmé in the tea room enjoyable and her adult ways and ideas a bit disarming ("I got up from my own chair, with mixed feelings of regret and confusion." p. 197), the true feelings of love engendered by Esmé are heightened by the nightmarish realities of his psychic disorder. Her parting words, " '. . . I hope you return from the war with all your faculties intact' " (p. 199) come back to him as he reads her letter. Once again he feels the love for both her and young Charles, and fondles the wristwatch that she has sent. The letter brings forth a sudden release from the enervating grip of his paralyzing disorder, and he feels a joyous relief in the need to sleep and relax. Indeed, he spells out the word "faculties" just as Esmé had spelled out the word "slain" to protect young Charles, showing us that just as Charles would not be hurt so he too would not succumb.

In Esmé Salinger has created a unique character. Old beyond her years, hiding behind "blasé eyes," Esmé confronts her problems with a ramrod poise and a discipline unknown to the writer. Although the narrator doubts her title, and

Esmé's own words build some doubts, we see that she is basically alone in the world and responsible for her very young brother. She is, despite her outward calm and control, a nervous girl. The narrator notices her chewed fingernails and damp hand, and Esmé nervously chews her cuticles when she discusses her "ideal" father. Esmé needs to love and be loved. She asks the narrator, "Are you deeply in love with your wife?" Without someone to love, she holds on to the remembrance of her dead father, who assumes noble proportions and who had a "'wife who could never have really understood him." The narrator, a writer, is amazed at Esmé's command of words, even those she misuses. In his own loneliness, he may see her desperate attempt to love someone real and to find that the love is returned. It becomes part of her dreamlike existence that she has made up a future to protect herself from the present reality. She trains herself "to be more compassionate" (p. 194), wants to grow up to make "heaps of money" singing jazz (p. 192), retire at 30, and live on a ranch in Ohio (p. 192). Undoubtedly, Esmé's outward dislike of Americans has not kept her from building dreams based on their conversations.

The narrator finds in Esmé a kindred spirit, a fellow searcher, and a love that is both ennobling and healing.

Setting

The war forms a natural background for a tale of loneliness, alienation, and redeeming love. The narrator meets Esmé on a dismal, rainy day just before he is to be shipped out to an uncertain future. In the second part, the uncertainty has become a reality; the dirt, despair, and depression have enveloped the narrator. It is against this backdrop that Esmé's love shines out.

Tone

As in most of his works, Salinger creates characters, mood, and feelings through the careful selection of words. Much of the narrator's feelings for Esmé hinge on the use of the word "squalor." Since she has just misused the word "prolific," the narrator is equally surprised at Esmé's comment, "I prefer stories about squalor." To his puzzled reply, she returns with, "Squalor. I'm extremely interested in squalor." (p. 197) However, when looking at Esmé's existence—a young, lonely orphan evacuated from war-torn London, responsible for a younger brother—the narrator and the reader can see that she really has nothing. Esmé is aware of this. Armed only with rigid self-discipline, a vocabulary, remembrances of a perfect father, and dreams for a beautiful future, she has built her life around searching for someone to love and be loved by.

The careful reading of words in the opening paragraphs reveals the narrator's true feelings for Esmé. He talks about his "breathtakingly level-headed girl" (Esmé was a beautiful dreamer), the decision (". . . we've decided against it . . ."), and the fact that he didn't get to see much of his mother-in-law any more. The words that he writes to "edify" Esmé's prospective groom become a story of unselfish love that saves a life.

Questions

1. What kind of person is the narrator?
2. What kind of person is young Esmé?
3. How does Esmé cope with the realities of her life?
4. In what ways does Esmé affect the narrator's life?
5. What does Salinger gain by using the word "squalor"?
6. Why does the story have two parts?
7. What purpose does the opening paragraph serve?

The Short Story in the Junior High School

The reading of short fiction in the junior high school serves three vital functions:

1. To offer students interesting, readable works that build an interest in literature.
2. To give the students an introduction to the art of short story writing and the act of literary creation in works of varying difficulty.
3. To build the skills needed to read more difficult works encountered in senior high school.

The beginning junior high school student often brings to class a minimal knowledge of literature but a wide range of reading interests in different fields. The skillful teacher will try to expand the narrow interests of some, curtail the expansive interests of others, and, at the same time, offer a selection of stories that has literary merit and interest. The ninth-grade English teacher often has a class with a wide range of reading levels, and it is here that the teacher must cope with reading levels and interests by individualizing instruction.

At the outset of a serious study of literature the student must not simply read pages or discuss only "what happened." The writer had a purpose and used judgments when creating the fiction. The students should read to find that purpose and discover the ways in which it has been achieved. They can then go on to develop their reactions and responses (affective learning) to the literature, perhaps building a viable critical mode of thinking.

The progression through the levels of junior high school should include specific cognitive learning in the area of short fiction. To discuss the short story meaningfully, the students should know how the terms of fiction, the various elements of the short story (plot, character, setting, theme, and diction), and be able to point out how they are used by authors whose works range from the simple to the sophisticated and complex. These skills should be started in the junior high so that students can handle more difficult works commonly assigned and anthologized in the senior high school.

"Night of Vengeance" by Paul Darcy Boles

Source: *Ten Modern American Short Stories* edited by David A. Sohn
Recommended level: junior high school

The Plot-Centered Story

"Night of Vengeance" can be read solely as an adventure story or as an adventure story with a statement about life. This statement deals with man's need for freedom and his never-ending struggle to achieve it.

The strong plot closely follows the pattern of the ideal plot line with (1) conflict, (2) rising action, (3) climax, (4) falling action, and (5) denouement or resolution. Plotted out, the story appears as follows:

1. *Conflict*—on the opening page we see Voldi's need for

freedom and his desperation as a galley slave.
2. *Rising action*—the hope for freedom continues to grow into action as:
   a. Bear tells of the slave insurrection at Actium.
   b. the ship is separated from others by battle and storm.
   c. the strangeness of the night becomes more noticeable.
   d. Bear's plan takes on new meaning.
3. *Climax*—Voldi decides to secure his freedom or die in the process.
4. *Falling action*—the plan is carried out.
5. *Denouement*—the discovery of the Star of Bethlehem is made and its effects mentioned.

With such a strong plot line in the story, the student should note how the other elements are used. The characters, as often happens in the adventure story, are thinly drawn. In this work the students should find the familiar types of (1) the hot-blooded youth aching for freedom, (2) the aged, philosophical strong man filled with quiet hope, and (3) the faceless, nameless opponents. Although Voldi is a stock character, he does change during the course of the story as his fiery rage is mellowed into an understanding of man's ways and a concern for justice is fostered by the author's interesting use of the light.

The setting becomes quite important as it supports the theme of man's freedom. This is accomplished by the use of contrast. The contrast deals with slavery and freedom. For example:
1. The time is the Roman domination of the civilized world and the period shortly before the birth of Christ, whose teachings set many men free.
2. Voldi sits shackled to his oars while noticing the freedom of the fish, sea animals, and birds.
3. The darkness of the ship is contrasted with the strange light.

Students should notice the many references to the mysterious light before it is revealed at the very end. They should note the words used when the light is described ("wonder," "strangeness," "gentle," "strong," and "serenity") and see how, reflected in it, Bear's eye ". . . blazed with life." (p. 128) It is the same light that changes the tone of the story from merely adventure and suspense to mystery and wonder.

Questions
1. What is the actual time of the story? How do you know?
2. How does the setting relate to the main character?
3. In what ways are the characters familiar ones?
4. What is the purpose of the light?
5. Why did the author choose this particular title?

"Planet of the Condemned" by Robert Murphy

Source: *Ten Top Stories* edited by David A. Sohn
Recommended level: junior high school

The Plot-Centered Story

"Planet of the Condemned" makes use of the high interest level of the science fiction story coupled with the surprise ending. Although it does not follow the typical plot line because of the ending, the story quickly presents a conflict in the two characters. Upon re-reading the story, students will see the foreshadowing in Moncrief's mental flashback to the mice episode of his youth. Since the ending is the important part of the work, the author deletes much detail and technical information found in science fiction and takes us quickly to the mysterious planet. Here, the action moves very fast. We see Moncrief's extreme plan and the final irony. It is this ending that provides us with a theme. Bozemann's fears and Moncrief's ironic end repeat the underlying idea that tampering with scientific and natural laws can bring unexpected results. The importance of the plot is evinced as the third person, omniscient author tells his tale. He provides us with everything we need to know, not what we would like to know.

The characters suffer in this tale. Many of the students, so well aware of modern astronauts and the nature of space ventures today, may challenge the characterizations. Indeed, the "good-guy/bad-guy" depiction is obvious. Moncrief is too clearly portrayed by the narrator, who repeatedly tells us that Moncrief is being "'sardonic" or mocking. His greed and self-interest come out plainly. Even his name sounds a little too much like the grief he causes. Students may rightfully wonder how such a man could have become a space traveler. His murderous plan at the end may seem too extreme for someone who wants to gain "all the credit." Bozemann, in turn, is ineffectually drawn—the fact that he has found a girl and wants to live for her sake is supposed to depict his finer traits! Students may also find that for a person with such philosophical thoughts about the consequences of space travel, Bozemann is extremely ineffective in analyzing his partner. Students should be encouraged to discuss the characterizations—pro and con—to see the problems, methods, successes, and failures that writers experience.

Science fiction often depends on the element of setting, and Murphy uses it both to build the suspense and to create the final irony. The clues of the genetic mutations resulting in extreme growth become clear on a second reading as we see the large moss, the colossal strawberry-like trees, and the endless forests. The suspense builds from the moment the rocket door opens and we first look at the strange, roseate planet to the final demise of the panic-stricken Moncrief.

Some students will enjoy the story for its "idea," some may not think it is "accurate" enough, while others may say it has been done before and since. The students' levels of sophistication in regard to the short story should appear in the different reactions. The aware teacher will use these reactions to build criteria for evaluating a short story on different levels—from the very low, simple emotional reaction to the much higher critical look at the author's purpose and his success or failure in achieving it.

Questions
1. Is the title an effective one? Why?
2. What material has been left out by the author? Why?
3. What contrasts are developed in the characters? How is this done?
4. What clues has the author used to prepare us for the end?
5. What are the specific properties or ingredients of science fiction that can be found in this story?

"A Field of Rice" by Pearl S. Buck

Source: *Ten Modern American Short Stories* edited by
David A. Sohn
Recommended level: junior high school

The Plot-Centered Story

Pearl S. Buck is a traditional storyteller who knows a great deal about her subject. She spins a story in which the strong, fast-paced plot is supported by thinly drawn but interesting characters who represent attitudes and ways of life. Unlike many authors, Miss Buck manages to bring out clear-cut themes that can be stated in different ways.

The title, "'A Field of Rice," represents the battleground—physically, historically, and emotionally. The story moves along quickly, and time is eclipsed in order to get to the resolution. The story line appears as follows:

1. the confrontation between Li and the townspeople
2. Wang Sun's appeal
3. Li's orders to change
4. Wang Sun's second appeal
5. the work of the new order
6. the great failure
7. Wang Sun's attempt to help Li.

The story is told simply as the third person, omniscient author tells us all we have to know.

The conflict between the old order and the new rests in the characters of Wang Sun and Comrade Li. It is not merely a conflict between age and youth but, more importantly, between love and duty. For Wang Sun and the others the land is like their own flesh and blood. It is an inheritance from their ancestors, whose words of warning and advice echo through the story. In Wang Sun the reader should find the apolitical man of the soil (note that he lives in an earthen hut) who has a love of the land, a perception of the world and people gained through working with nature, and a compassion for the moral sterility of Comrade Li. Wang Sun and his fellows, who have successfully farmed their own lands and have learned to trust and help each other, now find that the blind new order robs them of their land, their heritage, and their very humanity. However, Wang Sun cannot lose his compassion for Comrade Li, whose sense of duty has destroyed his moral and emotional well-being. The nobility and fierce pride of the peasant come through as Wang struggles to prevent Li from shooting himself, and the old man says, " 'Why should you kill yourself? You are Chinese, too!' " (p. 123)

Comrade Li, whose narrow eyes reflect his own vision and outlook, becomes a pathetic figure cut off from the past and having no future now that he has failed in his duty.

The theme of the story can be stated in a number of ways that depict the conflicts that exist in the story. These include:

1. the man of the soil (feeling) vs. the man of the desk (reason)
2. the individual vs. the system
3. experience and knowledge vs. power and change
4. moral responsibility vs. duty.

This work should give the student excellent practice in stating a theme and supporting it with elements from the story.

Questions
1. What contrasts are found in the story?
2. What kind of person is Comrade Li? Why is he this way?
3. What are Wang Sun and the townspeople like? What has shaped them?
4. Why did the author use this title?
5. In what way is this story meaningful today?

"Eight-Oared Crew" by Harry Sylvester

Source: *Twenty Grand Short Stories* edited by Ernestine Taggard
Recommended level: junior high school

The Plot-Centered Story

From their past experiences with sports fiction the students can develop "typical" plot lines for this genre. Most of them deal with the "good" team player who overcomes the challenges posed by the "selfish" or "dirty" player, the ragamuffin team of inexperienced players that unifies in time to beat the perennial champions, and the selfish player who sees the error of his ways and redeems himself by winning the crucial game for the coach. Sylvester goes beyond the stereotyped sports story and gives the reader a strong conflict plot in which the primary conflict—Kip Grant's need to win the race for Al Leyden and to preserve his family tradition of winning at Poughkeepsie—parallels the inner conflict within Kip as he fights an ingrained snobbery and sense of class distinction to accept his crew members and grow in the understanding of others.

In the first conflict the reader will find the stock situations of the inexperienced team, the school's reputation at stake, and the friendly coach whose job is threatened. In several examples of foreshadowing, Kip's earlier doubts about the crew's performance under stress are echoed by Kip's brothers who predict that the novice team will break up. Oddly, it is the brothers' mockery and snobbery, contrasted by Mary Adams' support and the meeting with Pete Kowalik's brother in his broken-down car that heighten Kip's conflict. As Sylvester points out about Kip, "Strangely, though, he felt once more his new kinship with the crew, a relation delayed and hastened by the attitude of his brothers and friends, by the chance meeting with Kowalik's brother, by Mary Adams' quiet words." (p. 51)

However, the test for Grant comes during the big race. When the crew predictably comes apart near the end of the race and loses a commanding lead, Kip is tempted to abandon the shell as the taunts of his brothers ring in his ears, and his own sense of shame and embarrassment are directed against the crew. But, he sees Mary Adams' pleading look and remembers the words of Coach Leyden, " '. . . bring them in right—for their sake and the school's . . . if not for anyone else's.' " (p. 52) Grant's climactic decision to remain, to save the crew's morale for a future that does not include his own, becomes the victory. He gains a better knowledge of himself and of others.

The strength of Sylvester's plot lies in the ending which avoids the "Hollywood" or miracle finale that belies the foreshadowing. Added interest is given to the theme by having Kip achieve a personal victory in defeat, which so often happens in real life.

Sylvester's characters are thinly drawn and represent the two classes (rich and poor) in the story. However, they are contrasted throughout to show the forces working upon Grant. His brothers with their yacht are more than offset by Kowalik in his old car, Mary Adams, and Leyden. Kip is caught in the middle, balancing tradition, mistrust, and class superiority against understanding, trust, and a sense of personal worth.

Details from the setting are used effectively as the river becomes a battleground for Kip. The school, the private dining room, the yacht, and the old car provide the background against which a vital decision must be made. Student experience should provide interesting comparisons and discoveries about the author's use of story elements and themes in the sports-centered story.

Questions
1. Why does the title omit the main character's name?
2. What elements of setting and character help provide contrasts in the story?
3. How does the author increase the tempo of the story at the end simply by the use of sentence structure?
4. What is the basic underlying idea behind the story?
5. In what ways is the story similar to, and different from, other sports stories?

"Bounty Hunters" by Don Trompeter

Source: *Ten Modern American Short Stories* edited by David A. Sohn
Recommended level: junior high school

The Setting-Centered Story

Although it is a major part of a short story, the setting is not ordinarily the major focus of a work, but rather a supportive element. However, a writer like Poe uses the setting to create a reaction of awe or shock that is often his main purpose. Other writers like the novelist Mary Ellen Chase or Mary Wilkins Freeman, the short story chronicler of New England types, use the setting as Trompeter does to influence and sometimes change the characters. The setting, as in London's "To Build a Fire" or Benet's "By the Waters of Babylon," overshadows the plot and characterization in "Bounty Hunters." We know very little about Jamie and Christian (an interesting name for a man who thinks a great deal about life and death) except that they hunt wolves for a living and they both long to spend the cold evenings at Christian's with his pregnant wife, Meda.

The setting dominates this story in three ways. First, in contrast to the ugliness of their job, as seen in the vivid description of Jamie's skinning of the black wolf, the beauty of nature and its sensuous appeal echo throughout the story. Second, the power and strength of the wolves seem to assert themselves in the face of the overpowering and inescapable tools of the bounty hunters. Finally, it is nature that makes Christian look at the day's work and reflect on the greater implications of life and death.

Students can find examples of nature's appeal in the following lines:

1. ". . . into the frost-aureoled sun, into the citrine flashing of color over the snow and the white-capped evergreen." (p. 140)
2. "The frost and sun and the bitter cold combined to set the world aflame. It was gold and saffron and pink and amber." (p. 141)
3. "The blown snow behind him on the lake was full of sun-gold, and the ravens were moving around the slain doe." (p. 144)
4. ". . . and the lake had taken on a pink and gray tone, and the tops of the distant pine flamed as if fired beyond the frost." (p. 148)

Despite the vivid description of the hunt and the ugliness of death, nature is seen as alive with the repeated "life" images of fire, the sun, and gold.

Although the wolves are no match for the hunters in their plane, the animals' power and strength are admired by Christian. He is annoyed when he tail-shoots them and has to finish them by hand. He feels the power of the black wolf's eyes and realizes that he can never destroy the light in its eyes. The running wolf becomes ". . . a blur of power and speed . . ." (p. 142), and, ironically, Christian comes to doubt his role in the killing. He sees the wolves' role in the natural order of life to be "an affirmation of the need to kill and to endure, which seems to rise from a primitive and universal grief that leaves one shaken with a sense of inexpressible isolation." (p. 141)

The day's work and nature's influence change Christian's thinking. Looking back at a buck nibbling on bark, he feels it will make a nice film. (p. 140) Later, missing a good shot, Christian disgustedly says, ". . . and knew I had Judas'd another beast for today, and had my fill of it." (p. 144) The change in attitude begins when Christian has to kill the black wolf up close with a handgun, and the following show of deepening concern for his role:

1. "His snarls coiled around those boulders like a whip around a man's soul." (p. 145)
2. At the bottom of page 145 he becomes aware of the life cycle in nature and its meaning to Man.
3. On page 146 he recalls the story of the dying Legionnaire who ". . . had witnessed the splendor of sunsets and storms, and clear night skies, and he related he had understood God."
4. ". . . tried to cleanse my hands of blood where no blood was visible, and cursed the paradoxes of life." (p. 147)
5. He refuses to shoot the fox because his "conscience" hurts. (p. 153)
6. He kills the small wolf at the end and says, ". . . but I did my duty, and he fell backward." (p. 154)

This change from the excitement of the hunt to a feeling of duty tinged with guilt marks the movement of the story. It leads the reader to the theme of the work which deals with the relationship between man and nature and the ultimate smallness of man set against the immensity of nature ("Somehow, a man seems to live only long enough to fulfill his own unique and trivial destiny." p. 154).

Questions
1. Where does the author achieve a good sense of realism in the story? Why does he accent this realism the way he does?
2. What contrasts can be found in the descriptions?
3. What changes, if any, take place in the hunters?
4. Why does Christian keep thinking of home? How does it fit into a repeated idea of the story?

5. What is the author saying to us about man and nature in this story?

"I Can't Breathe" by Ring Lardner

Source: *Twenty Grand Short Stories* edited by Ernestine Taggard

Recommended level: junior high school

The Character-Centered Story

For students accustomed to the adventure tale, the character-centered work poses problems. Conflicts may not be readily observable; action may be non-existent; changes in character may not occur. Then, students sometimes ask, why write a story just to tell us about a person? The answer, as students should come to see, is that the character in the story is most often a person like the reader—with problems, thoughts, sorrows, and joys. In the hands of a skillful writer the character can reach the reader, who just may see a little better into himself, or into others, after reading the work. The good writer interests us; the great writer affects us.

Ring Lardner's marvelous, daffy eighteen-year-old is a fine person to study in our look at the character-centered story. Students should find the devices and story elements used by Lardner to reveal her character traits. Speaking to the reader in the first person and through her diary, the charming, but vacuous, young woman reveals herself fully. Students will enjoy the portrait, and interesting comments can be made about Lardner's humorous look at the world of the lovesick. Among the traits revealed are the following:

1. The young woman is youth-oriented and can't appreciate her "old" aunt and uncle and finds it difficult ". . . to be left with old people that come to a place like this to rest." However, there seem to be quite a few interesting young folks available there. (p. 199)
2. She is boy-crazy. She can't stop juggling her five current and former boyfriends, and she has set two wedding dates and can't find a way of saying no to either of the two prospective grooms.

3. She is flighty. In a moment of despair, dreaming about the missing Walter, she notices boys sitting nearby. When one meets her the next day she writes, "... the cute one, came and sat right next to me and of course I didn't look at him. So we got to talking and he is even cuter than he looks ..." (p. 201)

4. She is highly irrational. Thoughts race through her mind at a dizzy pace, and most are based on sudden associations. Hearing a tune (she is extremely sensitive to all emotional impacts upon her senses) she writes, "and it seemed as if they must be playing it for my benefit though, of course, the person in that song is talking about how they miss their mother though, of course, I miss my mother too, but a person gets used to missing their mother and it isn't like Walter or the person you are engaged to." (p. 199)

5. She refuses to face up to reality or any responsibilities she acquires by being carried away by her feelings.

6. She is extremely emotional and throughout the entire work releases her anxieties in her favorite expression, "I can't stand it, I can't breathe, life is impossible." (p. 204)

After discussing the character, the students will probably agree that the other story elements of plot and setting are unimportant. However, most will enjoy the way in which the story is written. Lardner's skill is seen in his use of words. The young woman reveals herself and her thoughts, or lack of them, in her long, repetitious, illogical sentences and jumbled patterns of ideas. As she flits through the week, her mercurial emotional states, her fanciful flights, and her grand self-delusion are summed up in the masterful "I can't stand it, I can't breathe." Students should see the character development as a product of a masterful stylist and a humorous student of human nature.

Questions

1. How does the young girl reveal her character traits to us?
2. What are her most interesting traits?
3. Which ones are humorous, and which are not?
4. In what ways does the author reveal his knowledge of young people?
5. How does the written style of words and sentence affect the story?

"Antaeus" by Borden Deal

Source: *Ten Modern American Short Stories* edited by David A. Sohn
Recommended level: junior high school

The Character-Centered Story

Unlike the woman in "I Can't Breathe," the main character does not directly reveal himself to the reader. He shows his sense of responsibility by telling of his two acres of land and the calf that he takes care of. However, we learn about T. J. from the "I" person narrator of the story (first person, limited), who is one of the boys in the gang. From him, we learn that T. J. was:

1. fearless—he looked right at the boys with "pale blue eyes that looked washed out . . ." (p. 100)
2. independent—"His voice was resolute with the knowledge of his rightness . . ." (p. 100)
3. a leader—". . . we were all attracted by his stolid sense of rightness and belonging . . ." (p. 101)
4. intelligent—he knew when to give in to the boys and their wish to grow grass.

We also learn about T. J. from the author's interesting title, which is a key to the idea behind the story and the character. To help students understand these difficult allusions, you can familiarize them with the mythological dictionaries in the library or a good classroom source, such as J. E. Zimmerman, *Dictionary of Classical Mythology* (New York: Bantam Books, 1964). In Greek mythology Antaeus was a son of Poseidon (water) and Gaea (Mother Earth). He was a wrestler and engaged in a fierce battle with the mighty Hercules. During the contest Hercules was struggling to defeat Antaeus. He finally discovered that Antaeus renewed his strength whenever he touched the ground (gaining sustenance from his mother). Knowing this, Hercules defeated Antaeus by holding him over his head until Antaeus' strength had ebbed. In the story, T. J. is like the mythical Antaeus because he too gains strength and purpose from the soil. The narrator tells us, "He was a new Antaeus, preparing his own bed of strength." (p. 104) Later in the story, after the grass plot had been discovered and then destroyed by the boys, T. J.

". . . picked up a lonely blade of grass left trampled under our feet and put it between his teeth tasting it, sucking the greenness out of it into his mouth." (p. 109)

The story itself deals with a young, sensitive boy struggling for acceptance while struggling to renew himself in a world made barren and colorless (the tar roof). His intense love for the soil, which gives him both delight and a sense of worth, along with the feeling of independence, brings to the other boys a new-found respect for the beauty they create amidst the dreariness of their own surroundings.

Questions

1. What is the meaning behind the title? How does it affect the story?
2. Why isn't the story told from T. J.'s point of view?
3. What did T. J. bring to the boys?
4. Why did he run away at the end?

"A Mother in Mannville"
by Marjorie Kinnan Rawlings

Source: *Twenty Grand Short Stories* edited by
Ernestine Taggard
Recommended level: junior high school

The Character-Centered Story

Young Jerry is an unforgettable character whose sturdy self-discipline can overcome the deepest need to love and be loved. He displays a maturity and an understanding of love that goes beyond the older, more experienced narrator. In the surprise ending, the students should see that Jerry has created his "mother" to protect himself and the narrator from the pain of parting. He has succeeded in this as the narrator, so taken up with herself and her own feelings, relegates her concern to a passing interest by saying, ". . . his having a mother, any sort at all, not far away, in Mannville, relieved me of the ache I had about him." (p. 7) Indeed, the narrator's shock at the very end comes as a result of her own coldness, self-concern, and lack of insight into the needs of the love-starved youth.

Jerry reveals his sensitivity and need for love and acceptance by the protection he has built around himself. This protection is seen in his concern for gloves. He tells the narrator that, unlike many of the other boys, he has a pair to protect himself from the cold. (p. 1) Again the talk about his mother turns to sizes of gloves and the fact that he intends to buy his mother a pair. The students should see Rawlings' use of symbol in connection with Jerry's unstated needs. His need to be loved is shown when he talks about the dog finding him in the laurel patch: " '. . . when he found me, he acted crazy, and he ran around and around me, in circles.' " (p. 5) Jerry, too, needs to be found, not to be a foundling.

Jerry's deeds show that he is mature beyond his years, independent, responsible, and deeply sensitive. These traits are displayed when:

1. he wants to pay for the axe handle that broke,
2. he takes care of the dog and uses his own food when the lady arrives home a day late,
3. he feels the loss at the parting and withdraws to be by himself in the laurel, where he had achieved happiness before.

Finally, the author gives us an insight into Jerry's character through her observations and misconceptions. Laughing at his size, she later comes to say, " 'But you've done as much as a man.' " (p. 2) She is aware of his "very direct" eyes and his greatness of heart, although she cannot gauge the depth of his needs. Perhaps the goodness of Jerry is summed up by the narrator as she remarks, "As I spoke a light came over him, as though the setting sun had touched him with some suffused glory with which it touched the mountains." (p. 2)

Questions

1. Why did Jerry deceive the friendly woman?
2. Why was he able to deceive her so easily?
3. What do you suppose made her both angry and surprised at the end?
4. What kind of person was the narrator?
5. Why are "gloves" mentioned twice in this short story?

"The Schwartz-Metterklume Method" by Saki

Source: *50 Great Short Stories* edited by Milton Crane
Recommended level: junior high school

Tone and the Short Story

Students will have no difficulty in finding the overall tone in this delightful Saki story. Saki's humor and satirical touch are evident in the theme and characters. His familiar themes are obvious in the work and reappear in numerous other stories. They include:

1. the ageless struggle between imagination (honesty) stolidity (phoninesss), as in "Shredni Vashtar,"
2. the confrontation between youth and age, as in "The Lumber Room,"
3. the gullibility of people taken in by appearances, as in "The Open Window."

Lady Carlotta joins Saki's gallery of interesting characters who struggle against social snobbery, complacency, phoniness, and the lack of imagination. Using the familiar comic element of mistaken identity, Saki has Lady Carlotta take on and hopelessly outclass the Quabarls. A champion of the underdog and those in distress, Lady Carlottta comes to the aid of the four Quabarl children. (p. 330) In their conversations in the car and at the dinner table, Lady Carlotta attacks Mrs. Quabarl's self-assuredness by suggesting other makes of cars and wines to her. Then she exposes the woman's phoniness by claiming to use the famous "Schwartz-Metterklume" method of instruction. Finally, she attacks the Quabarls' snobbishness and sense of superiority by commenting about the outrageous antics of her "previous employers." The humorous history lesson, based on Mrs. Quabarl's demand for interest, becomes both a lighthearted spoof of educational methods as well as a comment on the relationship between parents and children.

In addition to the contrast between the adventurous, crusading Lady Carlotta and the laughable Quabarls, Saki achieves a tone of humor through his choice of words. Students must look closely and re-read or they will miss many tongue-in-cheek phrases or amusing descriptions. For example, Mrs. Quabarl is first seen as an "apparition," the town is immediately described by the "uninteresting length of the station," and Irene says the boys are after the "shabby women" (Sabine Women). As Lady Carlotta leaves the Quabarls, she is described as "the dismissed instructress of youth." Indeed, Lady Carlotta does teach us another Saki lesson about the foolish nature of people and the ways to get around them.

Questions
1. Where did Lady Carlotta get the "Schwartz-Metterklume Method"?
2. In what ways does Saki describe the characters?
3. In addition to the general plot line, how does Saki achieve a tone of gentle humor?
4. What is Saki trying to point out about people in this story?

"Clothe the Naked" by Dorothy Parker

Source: *Twenty Grand Short Stories* edited by Ernestine Taggard
Recommended level: junior/senior high school

Tone and the Short Story

In contrast to the humor of a Saki story, the unrelieved pathos of Dorothy Parker's story will provoke many emotional reactions ranging from sadness to a deep feeling of empathy. In presenting first the tribulations of the stoic, unbowed, heroic Big Lannie (truly an Earth Mother figure) and secondly the tragic experience of Raymond, the author has built her tone through pure narrative, contrast, and the power of her prose.

Dorothy Parker creates a deep feeling for Big Lannie by describing the unending tragedies she endures as life hurls one disaster after another at her. Stoically accepting physical pain as well as the ill-deserved insults of her employers, Lannie endures with her philosophy, "They had happened to her; there they were." (p. 90) Lannie's problems continue with her blind grandchild, Raymond. She fights the doubts of being able to take care of him, sacrificing (unweaving the mats late at night, begging for old clothes) to keep him from the dreaded institution.

The contrast between Big Lannie and her employers heightens the reader's feelings for the noble maid. Where she is loyal and selfless, they are haughty and selfish. Where she suffers through life at survival level, they ride through life blissfully unaware of pain. The consciousness of Mrs. Ewing with her "noble obligations" to her many causes and "things" contrasts with Lannie's giving of herself to Raymond. The most poignant use of contrast is the use of parallel scenes depicting Raymond's excursions into the street. Students can list the many joyous experiences of the first walk detailed by Parker's clear descriptive skills and contrast them with the singular horror of the second walk.

The feelings of horror, despair, and helplessness come to the reader during the description of Raymond's second walk. The students should notice Parker's careful building of Raymond's character and his optimistic outlook, despite life's hardships. Then, we are given a jolt as Raymond's joy is turned into terror and his world turns inward to the dark. Students will be puzzled by Parker's effective ambiguity— what exactly happened to Raymond? The repeated use of "it" to describe the force that attacks the helpless, blind youth will elicit different replies from the reader. For some, Raymond will have been attached by a dog ("... and it licked over him, howling higher." p. 97). However, others will note that the title encompasses more than just Lannie and Raymond. It signals the author's concern and compassion for all the suffering, poor, and helpless. These readers will feel that Raymond has been mauled by what Lannie has survived—the unending pain and suffering of life for those who have little to offer but their own strength and endurance. Raymond's only hope is the warm, comforting Lannie. But, Parker seems to suggest, what is Lannie's hope?

Questions
1. What kind of person is Big Lannie?
2. What is the relationship between Lannie and her employers? What causes this?
3. What kind of life does Raymond have with Lannie?
4. What happens to Raymond? How do you know?
5. Why does the author use this title?
6. In what way does the author use words effectively to

create movement in the story and to create reader reaction?

"Sucker" by Carson McCullers

Source: *Ten Modern American Short Stories* edited by David A. Sohn
Recommended level: junior high school

Tone and the Short Story

Carson McCullers' ability to catch the emotions and tensions of young people, particularly lonely young people, is clear in "Sucker." She captures the humor and pathos of growing up and searching for self-understanding. In this work the humor is overshadowed by the emptiness and sorrow that come to Pete, the narrator, as he sadly becomes aware that he has lost something with Sucker that can never be regained.

The tone of the work comes out of the basic ideas of the story. These include the passing of childhood (for Sucker) and the ignorance of youth that leads to an end of innocence (for Pete). These ideas are cleverly interwoven into the maturation of both boys, and a reversal occurs early in the story when Pete says, "The room was mine and I used it as I wanted to." (p. 88) At the end, after he has irrevocably alienated Sucker (who has now inherited Pete's mask of hardness and silent scorn), Pete sadly admits, "Our room isn't mine at all any more." (p. 97) Students will closely identify with Pete's plight as he says, "But everything is so different that there seems to be nothing I can do to get it right." (p. 98)

Readers should be able to pick out the keys to the story. They should be aware of the author's attempt to mold reactions from the reader by closely following the first person narrator. In Pete's words they should find the humor, confusion, and despair that make up the teen-ager's day-to-day life. The humor springs from Pete's ignorance of himself and the motives of others. Constantly reminding us of Sucker's gullibility, he fails to see that he is another sucker as Maybelle

Watts walks him over the coals of adolescent puppy love. Even his sad discovery, "Girls like her are hard to understand," (p. 93) screams out his unawareness of Maybelle. The harsh words he hurls at Sucker (p. 96) could be Maybelle's words directed at him. Pete, caught in the trauma of his first love affair, is painfully unaware of Sucker's own need to be accepted (" 'No matter what you did, I always knew you liked me,' " p. 91). Like the Ancient Mariner, Pete learns too late and is all the sadder for it.

Pete's treatment of Sucker will bring out sympathetic reactions and experienced frustrations from the students as they relate to the story. They will see how Pete selfishly uses Sucker as a sounding board amidst his own confusion. Realizing that Sucker is growing up, but wrapped up in himself and unable to give needed sympathy and assurance, Pete treats Sucker just as brusquely as Maybelle treats him. The sadness comes from the fact that while he can "adjust" to the loss of Maybelle, the resulting break with Sucker may be irreparable. The student will see that Sucker, at the end, is not the boy at the beginning, and the change is a sad one.

Discussions should involve the students in Carson McCullers' handling of the emotions of young people, and her humorous, simply-stated insights ("... and his [Sucker's] face had the look of a kid who is watching a game and waiting to be asked to play." p. 89) can serve as a springboard for the students' own descriptions of the problems of youth.

Questions
1. Why is the title appropriate for the story?
2. List the insights into young people that the author has caught in the story.
3. In what way is the point of view used important?
4. What makes this story universal in its appeal?

"A Turn with the Sun" by John Knowles

Source: *Ten Modern American Short Stories* edited by
David A. Sohn
Recommended level: junior/senior high school

The Over-All Story Analysis

John Knowles turns to his favorite subject—the emerging adolescent as he encounters the social pressures and demands of the private school—for this story of life and death. Subjecting his immature protagonist to these pressures, Knowles presents the inner conflicts that result from the need to be accepted and the problems that accompany maturation. This is set against the larger vision of the relationship between man's life and the endless cycle of nature's seasons. Knowles uses all the elements of the story—plot, character, setting, and diction—to bring out his themes in a powerful, unified work.

The plot is a strong one and uses the cyclical structure (as the seasons are cyclical) to bring out the relationship between Lawrence Stuart's tragic year and the accompanying turn of the seasons. The students will discover Knowles' careful, effective use of flashback and parallel scenes in a plot action line (see Fig. 7).

Although flashback takes us from September to April, the actual time of the story is between late afternoon on a beautiful April day and later that same night. Interestingly, Lawrence's fortunes follow the seasonal changes. The fall and winter bring isolation and despair while the emerging sun is accompanied by a new sense of life and reality for Lawrence.

The cycle is reinforced by two parallel scenes—Lawrence's visits to the school trophy room located in the gymnasium. These visits are important to the theme of maturation. In September Lawrence visits the room which is described as a "cool, sacred chapel." Lawrence is in a world of dreams and illusions based on ignorance and immaturity. In April, after scoring a winning goal for his lacrosse team but still not accepted by the others, Lawrence returns to the trophy room which is now a "chilly, damp chamber." He sees the futility of his attempt to be accepted on false grounds, and he gains a new awareness of himself. The gleaming trophy cup, the symbol of success in his narrower vision, is now a cup limited

Action Plot Line for Knowles' "A Turn with the Sun"

	Present		Past		
		I flashback begins			
Nature	early spring (April)		September (puzzlement)	December (anger)	February (contempt)
	the sun			no sun	no sun
Lawrence Stuart	crossing the bridge still not accepted		dive off the bridge fateful dinner at Devon Inn goes to trophy room	becomes strange isolates self	joins swim team ignores others unaccepted

Present

April
the sun
returns from successful game
goes to trophy room
dies at night diving from bridge

flashback ends

Past

April
the sun
loses girlfriend during vacation
acts worse at school
grades get worse

(Fig. 7)

by size, and he is ". . . a little amazed at this finiteness of the cup. . . ." (p. 27) Lawrence buries his false dreams during the second visit: "This room isn't a chapel at all, he thought with a passing wave of indignation, it's a crypt." (p. 28)

In the character of Lawrence Stuart, Knowles portrays the painful growth from immaturity to maturity. In his naiveté, Lawrence became a victim of his childishness, his lack of knowledge of people, his lack of self-discipline, and his tendency to base actions on false assumptions and dreams. From the beginning, he mistakenly relates social acceptance and school success to the Fullerton Cup, which becomes his Holy Grail (note how the room has a medieval quality with the banner-covered walls and gleaming silver). However, Lawrence's quest for this trophy is quickly ended because he cannot survive his vigil, the fateful dinner at the Devon Inn. Key statements that chronicle Lawrence's fall and expose his immaturity include the following:

1. ". . . it was as though his dive into the river had washed away his boyhood, and he stood clean and happy, wondering dreamily what he would be like now." (p. 15)
2. "Lawrence disliked and felt superior to Ging at once." (p. 16)
3. ". . . he felt himself more thoroughly aware than he had ever been of how the world went, of who fitted where, of what was grand and genuine and what was shoddy and fake." (p. 16)
4. ". . . he assumed every grown-up attitude he could find. All of it he brought forth, as an offering of fealty." (p. 18)
5. "Having missed the peak of his ambition, he assumed that lesser heights could be attained automatically." (p. 20)

Lawrence spends the bitter year in self-imposed exile and ironically comes to find a more meaningful answer to life just before his death. Like Pepe in Steinbeck's story, "Flight," Lawrence learns too late that ". . . the circle of the years changed things; it wasn't all up to him personally. . . . It was going to be a good summer." (p. 28)

Knowles builds the relationship between Lawrence and the seasons in the symbolic interpretations given to the story elements. The very title, "A Turn with the Sun," contains an ambiguity as it relates to the shortness of man's life as well as to the unending cycles of nature's seasons. The sun itself, with its warming rays, becomes a symbol of life, knowledge, and truth as described on the bottom of page 24, and it brings new life to Lawrence as ". . . the hot rays of the sun seemed to draw the rigidity out of his body. . . ." (p. 26) The trophy room, as discussed previously, is the crucible within which Lawrence is changed.

Finally, Knowles adds irony to the work. Lawrence achieves a quick success (his lucky dive) and then proceeds to fail miserably in his first opportunity at the Devon Inn. At the moment of his growth to inner peace and confidence he drowns, diving at night (unlike his daylight dive before all the others) for himself. It is also ironic that in death Lawrence has his picture placed on the gym wall, which, in his newly-found maturity, he would eschew.

Knowles uses his descriptive passages to build the sense of nature's beauty and the endless return to new life each spring. The story begins and ends, ironically, during the time of budding life. Knowles shows the beauty of life and nature in the appeals to the reader's senses. The very first sentence appeals to the sense of sight and touch ("exhilarating chill," "half-light," "dark green turf," "thick rug") while the beautifully lyrical last paragraph (pp. 30-31) captures the lasting glory and harmony of nature, contrasting it with the momentary glory of man:

> But the season moved on; that summer was the most beautiful and fruitful anyone could remember at Devon. Blossoms scented the air and hung over the river winding quietly through the playing fields. And the earth, turned full toward the sun, brought forth its annual harvest.

Questions

1. What kind of person is Lawrence Stuart? What was he seeking?
2. What mistakes and misjudgments did he make?
3. In what ways did Lawrence change during the story? What was the result?
4. Why does the author spend so much time describing nature?
5. What examples of irony appear in the story?
6. What is meant by the title of the story?
7. In what ways does Knowles create a unified, complete story?

"A Sense of Shelter" by John Updike

Source: *Ten Modern American Short Stories* edited by
David A. Sohn
Recommended level: junior/senior high school

The Over-All Story Analysis

In "A Sense of Shelter" John Updike returns once again to
his favorite locale, Alton, Pennsylvania, and a familiar subject—the travails of a young adult facing the hurts and insecurities of growing up. Updike presents the story of William
Young (note the last name and his childish nickname,
"Mip") coping with the strange pangs of an adolescent love
he knows little about. More deeply, the story concerns a
young man's groping toward maturity as he struggles to re-
tain his "sense of shelter" against the intruding realities of
life.

Updike presents the plot clearly, building through the
school day, wherein time is compressed, to the important dialogue between William and Mary (note the many images of
kingship and the Renaissance period as William, the king, is
"reborn" in the story). As the reader discovers more about
William's character and sees Mary developed through
William's eyes, the suspense builds up to the inevitable climax
when the immature and the very mature collide. The point of
view, ostensibly third person, limited, is essentially William's
as details of the building and the luncheonette are seen
through his eyes. The detailed scenes in the luncheonette, the
study hall, and after school in the newspaper room, show us
the contrast between William's clear view of people and place
and his ignorance of the realities behind relationships.

Although Updike builds his scene carefully and captures
the paradoxical moods of stifling boredom and frenetic confusion that dominate the typical high school, William dominates the story. The reader will come to see him as unathletic
("always picked near the last"), intelligent, observant, sensitive, supercilious, and very protected. From an early age
William has set up barriers behind which he can function.
The school itself has become his shelter, where he can carry
on like a king, secure in his work and in the teacher's mute
praise. This feeling of security is strengthened by the cold,

gray weather so that "... he felt they were all sealed in, safe; the colors of cloth were dyed deeper, the sound of whispers made more distinct, the smells of tablet paper and wet shoes and varnish and face powder pierced him with a vivid sense of possession." (p. 67) In addition, William likes the school most when it is empty. After completing his work in the study hall, unlike the others, he "... yielded his conscience to the snug sense of his work done, of the snow falling, of the warm minutes that walked through their shelter so slowly." (p. 73) Thus, protected and dreaming, William prepares to announce his love to the unsuspecting Mary Landis.

In contrast to William's naiveté and sheltered existence, Mary Landis is experienced, popular, defiant, hardened by life, and thoroughly aware of the realities and heartbreaks of love. We see her underlying character even though she is pictured by William through adoring eyes ("Wild stories were told about her; perhaps it was merely his knowledge of these that put the hardness in her face." (p. 69). The world of differences between them (from the flashback of her stealing his schoolbag in the second grade) seems summed up in her cheerful greeting, "Hi, Billy," which instantly demotes William from a senior back to the second grade.

However hard and experienced she is, Mary handles the confrontation with compassion and sensitivity. Secure in her feelings about love and aware of her own insecurities about life, Mary tries to get William to see his own ignorance of social realities. By the time they have descended to the main floor, William has fallen into a strange new world, about which he knows very little. The king has suddenly become the court jester in an awkward world where even the familiar radiator clearing its throat cannot offer any assistance or security. William is reduced to blurting out an inane marriage proposal while through his mind races "perhaps it was just his mother's idea anyway." (p. 78) William is in a hostile environment as Mary continues to counter his weak arguments, sidesteps his awkward attempt to kiss her, and suffers his insulting remark with grace. As she speaks to "Billy," Updike writes, "In his world of closed surfaces a panel, carelessly pushed, had opened, and he hung in this openness paralyzed, unable to think what to say." (p. 78) All Mary can do now is reveal the truth to William, " 'You never loved anybody. You don't know what it is.' " (p. 80)

As Mary walks away and William shamefully enters his

shelter once again, a change has occurred, although he is not fully aware of it. The release from embarrassment and Mary's piercing truth have created a sense of freedom. The building seems oddly strange. The heat is heavy, the "cloistered odors" no longer appeal to him, and he is afraid of being locked in for the night. Finally, into his empty locker "... his self seemed to crawl into the long dark space thus made vacant, the humiliated ugly, educable self." (p. 80) William, relieved of this terrible self, heads through the long, dark, tube-like hall to enter the outer, real world and, hopefully, be reborn.

Questions
1. In what way does the setting help reveal William?
2. What is William like?
3. What is Mary like as a person? How is she described?
4. Why does Updike use setting details again at the end of the story?
5. What are Updike's broader concerns in this story?

Part VII: COURSE OUTLINES

A major determination during the establishment of a mini-course/electives program involves the length of the course. Courses may vary from eight weeks to twenty weeks. Quite often the decision will be influenced by the length of the marking period, the school's total course offerings, scheduling procedures, district policies, teacher contracts, and staff capabilities, among others.

Suggested below is a sample outline for a ten-week mini-course, "Great Themes in Short Fiction." Since the class need for skills, both written and language, is best determined by the teacher at the time, the outline basically reflects literary works that have been grouped together to allow for a better transition of ideas. Works outlined below represent one way of setting up materials for a program.

There is more material listed than can be adequately covered during the time span given, especially if the instructor adds audio-visual materials to the course, but it is always easier to omit materials than to find new ones after planning has been completed. To lengthen the course, works should be added to the appropriate themes or new themes introduced to the course.

Where the minicourse idea is popular, but the seeming instability of the ten-week unit persists, the construction of a two-part, twenty-week elective might be considered. The flexibility of the minicourse provides many possibilities when the course itself is well planned and materials are carefully selected and prepared for teaching.

Great Themes in Short Fiction
Senior High School

Week #1	Week #2
Introduction to the Unit What is a short story? The traditional story— "The Tale"** The character sketch— "Theft"**	*Reviewing Elements of the Short Story* Setting—"The Outcasts of Poker Flat"* Character—"The Girls in Their Summer Dresses"* Plot—"The Shot"**
Writing Reviewing the well-written paragraph Reviewing the literary theme paper (theme statement and support)	*Writing* The character analysis literary theme Selection of extracurricular report (see IX)

Week #3	Week #4
Reviewing Elements Theme—"The Minister's Black Veil"** "The Phoenix"**	*Coping—Outside Forces* "By the Waters of Babylon"* "Soldiers of the Republic"* "The Masque of the Red Death"**
Writing The setting analysis literary theme	*Writing* The plot analysis literary theme

Week #5	Week #6

Coping—Outside Forces
  "To Build a Fire"*
  "The Lottery"**
	Coping—Others
	  "The Catbird Seat"**
	  "The Archimandrite's Niece"*
	  "The Bride Comes to Yellow Sky"*

Writing
  Using references in a literary answer (footnotes and bibliography)
	Writing
	  The research theme (library resources)

Week #7	**Week #8**

Coping—Others
  "Mr. Preble Gets Rid of His Wife"*
  "A Man of the World"*
	Coping—Self
	  "Silent Snow, Secret Snow"*
	  "The Old People"

Writing
  The theme analysis paper
	Writing
	  The theme analysis paper

Week #9	**Week #10**

Coping—Self
  "Young Goodman Brown"*
 	
Classroom presentation of reports
	Coping—Self
	  "For Esmé—with Love and Squalor"**
	
	Classroom presentation of reports

50 Great American Short Stories, M. Crane, ed.
**50 Great Short Stories*, M. Crane, ed.

Great Themes in Short Fiction
Junior High School

Week #1	Week #2

Introduction to the Short Story
    Elements of the story
    Purposes
    Methods of telling a story
 	
Classroom Reading of:
    "Michael Egerton"*
    "Polar Night"****
    "The Turtle"****
	Using Plot
	    "Night of Vengeance"*
	    "Planet of the
	    Condemned"****
	
	Writing Topics
	    1. There are several recognizable features of the plot-centered story.
	    2. A good plot suggests more than it tells.
	Student selection of short story reports (a 5-10 minute oral analysis of a work selected by the student)

Week #3	Week #4

Using Plot
    "A Field of Rice"*
    "Eight-Oared Crew"**
 	
Writing Topics
    1. Character is (or is not) developed carefully in the plot-centered story.
    2. Symbols or images often accomplish the author's purpose of bringing out theme or character.
	Using Setting
	    "The Masque of the
	    Red Death"***
	    "Bounty Hunters"*
	
	Writing Topics
	    1. Poe's use of setting differs from Trompeter's in several ways.
	    2. The use of setting often affects the development of character in a short story.

Week #5	Week #6
Using Character "I Can't Breathe"** "Antaeus"*	*Using Character* "The Catbird Seat"*** "A Mother in Mann- ville"**
Writing Topics The author's use of point of view is carefully chosen for a story.	*Writing Topics* 1. The humorous short story often is based on strong contrast or the unexpected. 2. The successful character is one who can change during the course of a story.
Week #7	Week #8
Building Tone "The Lottery"*** "The Schwartz-Metter- klume Method"***	*Building Tone* "Clothe the Naked"** "Sucker"*
Writing Topics 1. The surprise ending is successful when used correctly. 2. Successful satire depends on the knowledge of the reader and what the author chooses to observe.	*Writing Topics* 1. To successfully build tone the author uses several elements of a story. 2. Tone is very often the result of an author's use of one major element of short story.

Week #9	Week #10

Analyzing the Story
  "A Turn with the Sun"*
  "A Sense of Shelter"*
 	
Writing Topics
  1. The successful artist achieves a unity of effect in his short story.
  2. The theme of the successful writer is universal and goes beyond the immediate story.
	Classroom oral presentation of short stories and class discussion of student analyses

Part VIII: STRATEGIES FOR STUDENTS

Upon completion of any unit of instruction, the teacher should be concerned with (1) what the student has specifically learned, (2) how the individual student relates the ideas from the course to his own experiences, and (3) what material from the course the student takes with him once the books have been collected.

In order to measure what the student has learned as well as to evaluate the student's handling of written and language skills, the teacher should make available a series of Student Response Activities that relate in various ways to the materials covered during the units of study. To satisfy the differentiated learning abilities within the class, it is suggested that these activities be presented to the students in levels of difficulty. By doing this, the teacher may contract with the individual student for a specific response, or he may encourage the student to attempt topics from increasingly difficult levels. The experiences for this course provide both specific and more general literary topics that range from the easily organized response to the sophisticated, difficult reaction. As examples, the following activities are suggested:

Level A:

Student responses tend to be based on the reading of easier materials and more readily available research materials. The theme statement followed by unified paragraphs of support should be the organization goal for the written response.

1. Select one of the following writers and, after preliminary reading of at least 5-10 stories, develop a limited theme to support using (a) the works read and (b) appropriate research. The final theme will be written out in a clearly developed, well-supported paper.

O. Henry (William Sydney
    Porter)
Ring Lardner
Guy de Maupassant
Anton Chekhov

Saki (H. H. Munro)
Roald Dahl
Ray Bradbury
Washington Irving

2. Walter Van Tilburg Clark is a writer who uses nature in many of his stories. After reading a minimum of five stories, develop a written paper in which you discuss (a) Clark's views toward nature, and (b) the uses of nature in his stories that support these views.

3. From the topics listed below select one. After reading 5-10 short stories, write an outline of your ideas. After it has been accepted by the teacher, write a paper supporting your ideas with (a) the stories read and (b) appropriate critical material.

Edgar Allan Poe and the Unity of Effect
Bret Harte and the Local Color Story
From Dupin to Holmes: Characteristics of the Detective Story
The Beginnings—Short Stories of Washington Irving
Science Fiction and the Short Story

4. Write a character sketch of someone you know. In the sketch use the ideas and character description techniques you have seen in stories read in class. Be prepared to explain these techniques to the class.

5. Select three stories not read in class but by an author discussed during the course. For each story, write an analysis discussing (a) the author's purpose, (b) how this purpose was brought out, and (c) how the story was similar to or different from the author's work read in class.

6. Using a tape recorder, record a short story complete with characters, sound effects, and background music. Be prepared to have your tape played in class.

Level B:

Student responses tend to be based on more difficult reading material and more difficult research material. Creative assignments will demand greater insights into the subject and more time for a thorough development of the project.

1. The student will select one of the following writers and, after a preliminary reading of 5-10 stories, develop a limited

theme to support using (a) the works read and (b) appropriate research. The final theme will be written in a clearly developed, well-supported paper.

Ambrose Bierce	Somerset Maugham
Henry James	James Joyce
John Steinbeck	Katherine Mansfield
Nikolai Gogol	Eudora Welty
Sholem Aleichem	Joseph Conrad
Stephen Crane	Sarah Orne Jewett

2. The following authors are noted for their stories dealing with individuals. Select one author, read a minimum of five stories, and write a paper dealing with the author's purposes and techniques used in stories dealing with character revelation. The paper should contain your own ideas which may be supported by appropriate critical material.

Mary F. Wilkins Freeman	John Updike
Carson McCullers	James Joyce
Flannery O'Connor	Katherine Anne Porter

3. Writers often use mythological/archetypal themes, symbols, or allusions in order to strengthen their themes or characters. Read the stories below (they can be found in a general collection of short stories) and show how each writer has used mythological/archetypal elements in his or her story.

"Leiningen Versus the Ants," Carl Stephenson (concept of the hero)

"Eve in Darkness," Kaatje Hurlbut (allusions)

"A Worn Path," Eudora Welty (the quest and numerous allusions)

4. From the topics listed below select one. After reading 5-10 short stories or doing the appropriate research, write an outline of your ideas. After the outline has been approved by the teacher, write a paper discussing your ideas with clear support from your stories or from the research that you have done.

Major Symbols in Hawthorne's Short Stories

The "tutor" and the "tyro" in Hemingway's Short Stories

The Artist and the Short Story—Techniques of Henry James

The Search and the Suffering—Themes in the Short Fiction of F. Scott Fitzgerald

The Inner Man—A Look at Sherwood Anderson's *Winesburg, Ohio*

Contemporary Black Short Fiction

The Gothic Short Story

Naturalism and the Short Story

Man and Machine—Ray Bradbury Themes

5. Using someone familiar to you, write a character sketch in which a basic trait of the character is highlighted. Then, after finishing the sketch, develop a short *fictional* character sketch based on your original. Be careful to separate the fact from the fiction and be prepared to read both to the class.

6. Using a camera, take a series of pictures that would serve as focal points for a short work of fiction. Then create a display using these pictures and, under each, write the ideas suggested by the picture for a possible story. Be prepared to display your work to the class.

7. Keep a journal for one week in which you collect your thoughts, pictures of an interesting person, or dialogue overheard. From these entries create a short short story. Be sure that you carefully arrange, select, add, or change elements to make a good fictional work.

Part IX: TEACHER READING LIST

There are many books of critical analysis and literary background to be found in the library under the individual author's name. The following books deal with the art of short fiction and critical approaches to the short story. They may provide the teacher with new insights, suggest areas for student research, and indicate subjects to be developed during the course.

Birnbaum, E. *Guide through the Romantic Movement.* New York: The Ronald Press Company, 1942.

Boynton, R. W. and M. Mack. *Introduction to the Short Story.* New York: Hayden Book Company, 1965.

Brace, G. W. *The Stuff of Fiction.* New York: W. W. Norton & Company, Inc., 1969.

Brooks, C. and R. P. Warren. *Understanding Fiction.* New York: Appleton-Century-Crofts, Inc., 1959.

Burnett, W. and H. Burnett. *The Modern Short Story in the Making.* New York: Hawthorn Books, Inc., 1964.

Curry, P. S. *Creating Fiction from Experience.* Boston: The Writer, Inc., 1964.

Daiches, D. *Critical Approaches to Literature.* Englewood Cliffs, N. J.: Prentice-Hall, Inc., 1956.

Defalco, J. *The Hero in Hemingway's Short Stories.* Pittsburgh: The University of Pittsburgh Press, 1963.

Dickson, F. and S. Smythe, eds. *Handbook of Short Story Writing.* Cincinnati: Writer's Digest, 1970.

Feidelson, C. *Symbolism and American Literature.* Chicago: The University of Chicago Press, 1953.

Feinberg, L. *Introduction to Satire.* Ames: The Iowa State University Press, 1967.

Hildick, W. *Thirteen Types of Narrative.* New York: Crown Publishers, 1970.

Kempton, K. P. *The Short Story*. Cambridge: Harvard University Press, 1966.

Matlaw, M. and L. Lief. *Story and Critic*. New York: Harper & Row, 1963.

Pattee, F. L. *The Development of the American Short Story*. New York: Biblo and Tannen, 1923.

Roberts, E. V. *Writing Themes about Literature*. 3rd ed. Englewood Cliffs, N.J.: Prentice-Hall, Inc., 1973.

Rohrberger, M. *Hawthorne and the Modern Short Story*. Paris: Mouton & Co., 1966.

Schorer *et al.*, eds. *Criticism: The Foundations of Modern Literary Judgment*. New York: Harcourt, Brace & World, Inc., 1958.

Summers, H., ed. *Discussion of the Short Story*. Boston: D. C. Heath & Company, 1963.

West, R. B. *The Short Story in America 1900-1950*. New York: Regnery, 1952.

West, W. *On Writing, By Writers*. New York: Ginn and Company, 1966.

ABOUT THE AUTHOR

Currently Chairman of the English Department at John F. Kennedy High School, William G. Swenson holds his M.A. in English from New York State College for Teachers, Albany, and his M.S. in Secondary Administration from Hofstra University. He has been teaching English for many years and is presently involved in writing a novel for junior-senior high school students. Also, Mr. Swenson is the author of Bantam's *The Mythmakers, Guide to Minicourse/Electives Programs, The Search for Values through Literature, Sports in Literature,* and is currently working on *Great Themes in Drama.*

BANTAM'S ELECTIVE-BOUND PROGRAM
SAVES YOU VALUABLE HOURS

Hours spent researching and structuring an elective area, setting up goals, objectives, activities, selecting titles.

With **every** program, you get 3 different teacher's guides, 36 books, a display case, and 30 Reading Response Cards—all geared to help you teach electives easily and effectively.

For complete information, use the handy coupon below and teach an elective your students will enjoy and remember.

———————

If you're teaching the short story,
you'll want to know more about—

GREAT THEMES IN SHORT FICTION.

And you might be interested in—

>THE ADOLESCENT IN LITERATURE
>THE MYTHMAKERS
>SEARCH FOR VALUES
>SPORTS LITERATURE
>SCIENCE FICTION
>THE PIONEER SPIRIT
>VALUES AND RELIGION
>PSYCHOLOGY AND AWARENESS
>ROLES AND RELATIONSHIPS
>NEW APPROACHES TO WRITING
>COMMUNICATIONS AND MEDIA
>FUTURISTICS: SEEING TOMORROW TODAY

- -

☐ Please send me more information on Bantam's new Elective-Bound Program.

Name_____

Address_____

City_____State_____Zip_____

Send to: **LEARNING VENTURES,**
A Division of Bantam Books, Inc.,
666 Fifth Avenue, New York, N. Y. 10019.

GTSF

START A COLLECTION

With Bantam's fiction anthologies, you can begin almost anywhere. Choose from science fiction, classic literature, modern short stories, mythology, and more—all by both new and established writers in America and around the world.

☐	75 SHORT MASTERPIECES: Stories from the World's Literature Roger B. Goodman, ed.	2102 ●	95¢
☐	THE WORLD'S BEST SHORT SHORT STORIES Roger B. Goodman, ed.	6382 ●	95¢
☐	50 GREAT AMERICAN SHORT STORIES Milton Crane, ed.	6893 ●	$1.50
☐	THE NICK ADAMS STORIES Ernest Hemingway	7250 ●	$1.75
☐	TEN TIMES BLACK: Stories from the Black Experience Julian Mayfield, ed.	7351 ●	95¢
☐	50 GREAT HORROR STORIES John Canning, ed.	7601 ●	$1.50
☐	THE MARTIAN CHRONICLES Ray Bradbury	7900 ●	$1.25
☐	TIMELESS STORIES FOR TODAY AND TOMORROW Ray Bradbury, ed.	8162 ●	95¢
☐	50 GREAT SHORT STORIES Milton Crane, ed.	8192 ●	$1.50
☐	WE BE WORD SORCERERS Sonia Sanchez, ed.	8347 ●	$1.25
☐	TEN MODERN AMERICAN SHORT STORIES David A. Sohn, ed.	8571 ●	95¢
☐	THE BALLAD OF THE SAD CAFE AND OTHER STORIES Carson McCullers	8596 ●	$1.25
☐	TWENTY GRAND SHORT STORIES Ernestine Taggard, ed.	8609 ●	95¢
☐	DEVILS AND DEMONS Rod Serling, ed.	8790 ●	95¢
☐	TEN TOP STORIES David A. Sohn, ed.	8791 ●	95¢

Buy them at your local bookstore or use this handy coupon for ordering:

Bantam Books, Inc., Dept. EDF, 414 East Golf Road, Des Plaines, Ill. 60016

Please send me the books I have checked above. I am enclosing $_____ (please add 35¢ to cover postage and handling). Send check or money order —no cash or C.O.D.'s please.

Mr/Mrs/Miss_____

Address_____

City_____State/Zip_____

EDF—7/75

Please allow three weeks for delivery. This offer expires 7/76.

WE'RE AWARE OF YOUR NEEDS.
AND PREPARED TO FILL THEM.

Bantam's Practical Teaching Guides to Minicourse Electives Programs have been designed for both today's teachers and their students. With each Guide, you can plan the courses that are right for you.

Effective programs don't just happen—you make them happen. And we'll make it easier.

- [ ] TEACHING TOMORROW TODAY: A GUIDE TO FUTURISTICS,
  Ronald T. LaConte   (Q2002—$1.25)
- [ ] A GUIDE TO CONSCIOUS COMMUNICATION,
  Judith Kahn   (Q2003—$1.25)
- [ ] GUIDE TO SCIENCE FICTION:
  EXPLORING POSSIBILITIES AND ALTERNATIVES,
  Doris M. Paine & Diana Martinez   (P2026—$1.00)
- [ ] THE LEADER'S GUIDE TO SOCIAL ACTION,
  Doris M. Paine & Diana Martinez   (P8001—$1.00)
- [ ] THE CREATIVE TEACHER (Language Arts),
  Edited by William Evans   (Q8007—$1.25)
- [ ] GUIDE TO MINICOURSE/ELECTIVES PROGRAMS,
  William G. Swenson   (P8008—$1.00)
- [ ] THE CLASSICAL MYTHMAKERS, William G. Swenson   (P8227—$1.00)
- [ ] THE ADOLESCENT IN LITERATURE, William G. Swenson   (P8228—$1.00)
- [ ] THE CREATIVE SOCIAL SCIENCE TEACHER,
  Edited by Paul H. Tedesco   (Q8281—$1.25)
- [ ] NEW APPROACHES TO WRITING:
  AN IDEABOOK FOR TEACHERS AND STUDENTS,
  Edited by Philip Werber   (Q8285—$1.25)
- [ ] A GUIDE FOR PARENTS: HOW TO RELATE TO
  SEX EDUCATION PROGRAMS, Eric W. Johnson   (P8286—$1.00)
- [ ] GUIDE TO THE SUBJECT OF SEX, Eric W. Johnson   (P8287—$1.00)
- [ ] SPORTS IN LITERATURE, William G. Swenson   (P8289—$1.00)
- [ ] PSYCHOLOGY: AN EXAMINATION OF HUMAN AWARENESS
  AND SELF-CONCEPT, Doris M. Paine & Diana Martinez   (P8290—$1.00)
- [ ] RELIGIOUS THOUGHT: AN EXAMINATION OF SPIRITUAL VALUE
  SYSTEMS, Doris M. Paine & Diana Martinez   (P8291—$1.00)
- [ ] THE SEARCH FOR VALUES THROUGH LITERATURE,
  William G. Swenson   (P8292—$1.00)
- [ ] GUIDE TO ANTHROPOLOGY: A NEW APPROACH,
  Margaret S. Hunt   (P9750—$1.00)
- [ ] GUIDE TO THE LITERATURE OF THE AMERICAN WEST,
  Doris M. Paine & Diana Martinez   (P9785—$1.00)
- [ ] GREAT THEMES IN SHORT FICTION: A PRACTICAL
  TEACHING GUIDE, William G. Swenson   (Q9786—$1.25)

BANTAM BOOKS, INC., SCHOOL & COLLEGE DIVISION,
666 Fifth Avenue, New York, N. Y. 10019

Please send me the Guides I have checked above. I am enclosing $_____
Send check or money order. No currency, stamps, or C.O.D.'s.

Name and Title_____

School_____

Address_____

City_____State_____Zip_____

FS-86